4-18-86
15.75

D0919600

479198

The Executive's Guide to Meetings, Conferences, and Audiovisual Presentations

The Executive's Guide

James R. Jeffries
Jefferson D. Bates

McGRAW-HILL BOOK COMPANY

*New York St. Louis San Francisco Auckland
Bogotá Hamburg Johannesburg London
Madrid Mexico Montreal New Delhi
Panama Paris São Paulo Singapore
Sydney Tokyo Toronto*

to *Meetings, Conferences, and Audiovisual Presentations*

CENTRAL MISSOURI
STATE UNIVERSITY
Warrensburg,
Missouri

Library of Congress Cataloging in Publication Data

Jeffries, James R.
   The executive's guide to meetings, conferences, and audiovisual presentations.

   Bibliography: p.
   Includes index.
   1. Meetings.   2. Meetings—Audio-visual aids.
3. Communication in management.   I. Bates,
Jefferson D., date.   II. Title.
HD30.3.J43   658.4′56   82-6567
ISBN 0-07-004060-5   AACR2

Illustrated by Ben Thomas

ISBN 0-07-004060-5

234567890   DOCDOC   8987654

The editors for this book were William Sabin and Christine Ulwick,
the designer was Naomi Auerbach, and the production supervisor
was Teresa F. Leaden. It was set in Souvenir Light
by University Graphics, Inc.

Printed and bound by R. R. Donnelley & Sons Company.

Contents

How About Stage Fright?
Voice Effectiveness
Sold to the Highest Bidder

11 *Running the Show*

Keeping Audience Interest
The Attention Span
Planning for Participation
A Twelve-Step Checklist

12 *Telling Your Story with Pictures*

What's Your Message?
Which Comes First, the Picture or the Word?
Storyboards Help Keep Your Thoughts Straight
Story into Pictures—the First Step

13 *Turning Words and Pictures Into a Polished Slide Presentation*

Get Out the Scissors

14 *Using Storyboards to Build a Smooth Presentation*

Making Your Creative Thinking Easily Understood
Storyboards
Display Boards

15 *Getting Your A/V Act Together Mechanically*

"Fine-Tuning" Techniques
Dressing Up the Slide Presentation
Temporary Handmade Slides
Buying Slides
Dropping Slides
81 Slides in an 80-Slide Tray
Mechanically Operated Programs
Multiscreen Presentations

16 *Multiscreen, Multimedia, and Multi-Image Presentations*

Just Scratching the Surface
In the Beginning, There Are Storyboards
Two-Screen Presentations

Three-Screen Presentations
Multimedia and Multi-Image Shows—Costly but Dazzling!
Recommended Reading

23 Summing up — 189

Foreword

Meetings, meetings, meetings!

It's been estimated that some 11 million meetings are held every day across this country. If indeed this is a truism, that's a lot of time, talent, and effort expended in group communications.

For those of us in human resource development (HRD), the training meeting is a sizeable investment of our budgets. Cost-effective meetings are a must, but you need think back only to a recent meeting you've attended (or perhaps conducted!) to realize we sometimes miss the mark.

From two very experienced and very knowledgeable people, here is, finally, a no-nonsense approach to this important field we call meeting planning. You'll find their straightforward treatise of our growing field a very readable and workable one.

With a vast array of experience to draw from, Jim Jeffries and Jeff Bates share those incidents and activities with even an occasional war story thrown in for good measure. Whether you're a novice or a veteran planner, this book will assuredly offer you some time-saving and money-saving tips.

It's a book for practitioners, written by practitioners. I know you'll learn from it.

EDWARD E. SCANNELL
1982 President, American Society for Training and Development
Director, University Conference Bureau, Arizona State University
Member, Meeting Planners International

If you cannot say what you have to say in 20 minutes, you should go away and write a book about it.

—LORD BRABAZON

Preface

How do two people write a book together? Frankly when we started this one, we weren't quite sure. Maybe we still aren't. But somehow everything has worked out.

Time and distance were occasional problems and many things have changed since we began our work; for instance, we both formed our own communication companies—Jeff's in the Washington, D.C. area, Jim's in Houston—but we have both stayed with it, conducting meetings ourselves as we wrote about the subject.

Another problem we had to resolve early in our joint effort was when and where (and how) to use the editorial "we." At first the solution seemed easy—for uniformity we would, as joint authors, simply use "we" throughout the manuscript. As the work progressed, however, we discovered that nothing is ever that simple. After all, each of us have had different experiences, but our knowledge and our specialties often overlap. In those parts of the book, we each took an independent shot at the subject matter, then exchanged and edited each other's copy. Those chapters represent truly joint efforts. Often we can no longer tell where one of us started and the other left off. Occasionally, one or the other of us would be the "sole source" of a particular item of information. In those cases, the writer used the singular "I." The choices have been made deliberately; we trust that after this explanation, you won't find them unduly confusing.

From our standpoint, we've enjoyed the collaboration and think combining our various experiences has resulted in a better book than one singularly written. We hope you feel the same way.

Acknowledgments

In a number of places in the text, we mention various people who have given us ideas for materials we included. Our sincerest thanks to all of them—Lee Beckner, Bud Rebedeau, Clem Roether, Jim Shattuck, Chuck Waterman, and Burt Wolder.

In addition, there were a number of people who were not mentioned who deserve a hearty thanks:

Ben Thomas, in our opinion, is the best design artist in the southwestern United States. Most readers have seen his work at one time or another in advertisements, corporate logos, or the Smithsonian Institution. The art and design in this book are products of Ben's creativity. Assisted by Max Alzina and J. R. Thomas, Ben produced all of the illustrations.

Lou Hampton, Jeff's partner and executive vice president of Hampton, Bates and Associates, Inc., is a nationally known seminar leader who frequently gives seminars on effective presentations. He has contributed a number of valuable suggestions at various stages of our work. More important, he actually tested much of the material set forth in this book in his own seminars.

For Chapter 20, "Professional Tips on Making Slides," Norm Arnold was our first choice for content editor. Fortunately, he was willing and helped clear up some sticky problems. In general, because of Norm's help, the readers are getting a much better chapter than the one originally drafted.

Katherine Jo Mannes, a consultant in reading and writing skills, and Jan Hunter, who works as a professional editor for a legal firm, volunteered to read our manuscript from a lay point of view and make editorial suggestions; both were extremely helpful.

Krystyna Jeffries deserves a very special thanks for her help in handling the myriad of detail attendant to preparing the text of this book.

Thanks also to Jodi Hester and Sue Price of Hampton, Bates and Associates for their always cheerful assistance, even when the final crunch was on; and to Mary Raitt, a professional researcher who helped us in compiling what we hope and believe to be the most complete bibliography of its kind ever assembled.

JAMES R. JEFFRIES
JEFFERSON D. BATES

If you don't know where you are going, you will
probably end up somewhere else.
                                    —LAURENCE J. PETER

Introduction

A well-planned, well-presented meeting is a wonderful communication tool. It helps you put your message across, in person, with the impact of a stage play tailored to an individual audience.

Unfortunately, there is another side to the coin. Poorly done, a meeting can be total agony for both the presenter and the audience.

Our objective in writing this book is to give information that will keep the meeting planner's task as painless as possible while ensuring that the audience will get the type of meeting it deserves—well-planned, well-presented, and consequently, well-received.

Conferences and meetings are big business. In the Washington, D.C. metropolitan area alone, well over a hundred companies make a full-time business of helping other organizations put on conferences and meetings. If your company has a budget that permits you to hire the expert services of such a firm, good for you. (Even so, we suggest you keep right on reading this book; it can still help you because it's designed to give you an insider's view of what goes on, and you'll be much better equipped to assess whether the firm you have employed is doing the best possible job for you.)

While we recognize that we can't be all things to all people, we have endeavored to write this book for just about everyone. From time to time, virtually any person sufficiently motivated to read this book must conduct meetings. Depending on your business or social involvement, these meetings could be for a handful of people—or for an audience of a thousand or more. Either way, be aware that many of the basic techniques of good meetings are the same, regardless of the size of the audience. Careful preparation, familiarization with props, good visual support, a knowledge of the audience, a tailored script, adequate rehearsal, and a solid presentation—all these items are essential.

Technicalities change by number of attendees, the amount of audience participation required, and the length of the meeting (multiday convention, for instance), and the complexities multiply as the requirements grow.

All meetings have a certain element of "you have to have been there to fully appreciate what happened." In other words, there is no substitute for experiencing things at first hand. In this book, we'll be sharing some of our experiences as we cover the techniques of good meeting planning. Owing to the limitations of space, we can give you only samplings of the technicalities.

Within these constraints, we have sought to include enough detail (in *most* of the areas involved in putting on meetings, conferences, seminars, and presentations) to permit our readers to do a creditable job *without consulting any other sources*. But admittedly, some of these areas are large enough to require entire books in themselves, so we have had to draw the line more often, and more tightly, than we would have liked. (Within the next couple of years, we hope to put together in another book a lot of new information we haven't been able to squeeze in here.)

We have put in many "inside tips" growing out of our combined practical experience—things you are unlikely to find in any other books. We believe that even oldtimers and hardnosed pros will find in these pages at least a few things they didn't know about before.

For readers who already know the basics, but are still relatively new at the game, we are furnishing the most nearly complete bibliography and source listing that the two of us, along with Mary Raitt (a professional researcher), could gather. Use this information to augment this book; there should be very few questions that you won't be able to answer.

The Executive's Guide to Meetings. Conferences. and Audiovisual Presentations

Why Hold a Meeting?

There's always an easy solution to every human problem—neat, plausible, and wrong.

—H. L. MENCKEN

Three Good Reasons Not to Hold a Meeting

Do you *really* want to have a meeting? Why? That's the first question you should ask yourself. Why, indeed?

Meetings are costly in *time.* They are costly in *money.* And they are costly in *indirect ways* that are often at least partially overlooked. In our experience, these hidden costs are rarely calculated except by the most knowledgeable leaders.

Among the obvious costs are:

- The participants' travel and lodging
- The rent on the hall
- The honoraria for outside speakers and presenters

Now let's look at some of the *hidden* costs that perhaps you hadn't thought about:

- The expense of the salary and benefit package of every person participating in the meeting; these are continuing costs for the employer, who would otherwise be paying the employee for the same number of hours on the job
- The cost of not doing, on time and on schedule, the things that the meeting participants should have been doing

The Big Question—Can You Do It Cheaper?

Surely there must be a cheaper way than a meeting to get your message across.

Think about it. Long and hard. If you can come up with another way that's as effective, as efficient, but cheaper—then *do* it. But don't be too quick to decide. In your deliberation about cost, never forget that some things are best learned in groups—through interaction with other people.

That's right. To improvise a bit of philosophy from a famous remark by Abraham Lincoln, meetings must have their good points, or smart managers wouldn't have so many of them.

So far we've been getting the bad news out of the way. Now we joyfully unveil the good news. Here goes:

ALL the costs mentioned in the bad news become insignificant if the meeting has a lasting positive effect on the participants.

And—the key to producing that lasting positive effect can be summed up in one word: *preparation.*

That's what this book is all about—how to plan and prepare meetings so that you, as a leader, can effect change.

Meetings Can Make Things Happen

In today's business society, no skill is more important—and more needed—than that of being able to transmit ideas effectively to groups of people. Without that skill, nothing changes; everything stands still. If (as a well-known political malaprop artist once put it), we "let the status quo stay just the way it is," we could all get left in yesterday.

We don't want this to happen, nor do you. Nostalgia is fine in its place, but we're old enough to remember some of the good old days that weren't all that great. Even though we know that not all changes are for the better, we can recognize the simple truth that if we don't keep trying to do better, we are inevitably going to do worse. So we won't guarantee that, simply by reading this book, you can keep from being left behind. We *will* guarantee, though, that if you employ the techniques we describe, you will become a more effective meeting planner and leader. And in the process, you'll establish yourself more firmly as an all-around leader. (We say "more firmly" advisedly. You are either already a leader, or are well on your way to becoming one, or you wouldn't be investing time and effort in studying ways of improving your skills.)

Okay, since you obviously don't need a sermon or a pep talk, let's get right down to cases.

Five Types of Meeting

As mentioned earlier, the key to effective meetings is *preparation*. Without that, meetings are dead—and deadly. But before you can begin to prepare, you must know exactly *what type of meeting you are planning, and what you want the meeting to do for the participants and for you.*

Generally, meetings are conducted to do one or more of the following:

- Inform
- Train
- Inspire
- Solve problems
- Resolve conflict

Finally, there are quite often combinations in which several, or even all of these purposes are addressed within the same framework.

Everything you do in the meeting should be directed toward getting your message across. If you carefully center all your preparation on that goal, you can be sure that your meeting will become a highly cost-effective method of transmitting your intended message.

But before we go into the "how-to" aspects of meetings, let's examine the different types more closely, and establish some uniform terms to ensure we're all tuned to the same wave length.

What Constitutes a Meeting?

In our book, a meeting is any occasion on which you as a speaker formally attempt to convey an idea, face-to-face, to a group of two or more persons. (And, even though we use here the term "face-to-face," we should point out that many of the same staging and speech techniques are applicable in other forms of mass communication—most specifically, television.)

You may not have thought about this before, but as you read this book, we suggest you check the points we make against the techniques you see being used on the tube. If you suppose that "Good evening, my fellow Americans" is not a carefully studied phrase intended to create a warm prologue, focusing your attention on the speech that follows, then we suggest you reconsider the words carefully—first one at a time, then all together.

The meeting to inform. A meeting to inform may be as simple as explaining to a few coworkers a new procedure or a new program. Or it may be as complicated as explaining to the nation how and why the first U.S. astronauts landed on the moon. Generally, your meetings will fall somewhere in between, but the basic techniques of presentation remain the same.

A meeting to inform has but one purpose: *to get the word out.* If you don't expect the attendees to develop a new skill or put a complicated procedure in place, you need only to present the message. If possible, do it *graphically.* Also, if you can manage to get some audience participation, that's commendable, but you don't necessarily *have* to have it. After all, your responsibility as the meeting leader is simply to pass along the information.

But, if you expect more than simple understanding from the people who attend—for example, if you intend for them to start using a totally new system or technique, then you must plan a more elaborate approach; put some *training* and *participation* into your meeting.

The meeting to train. The meeting to train can take a variety of forms. First, it can consist of pure training, the sole purpose of which is to teach a new skill. To most professional meeting leaders, however, this limited view seems wasteful. In the real world, if you are gathering people together, you will probably want to take advantage of the occasion to do a bit more. The training, however important it may be, is usually basic to a larger purpose. In any case, whether or not you decide to broaden the scope, you *must* make sure to incorporate at least certain essential features into your presentation.

Remember that people gather knowledge through their physical senses—primarily seeing and hearing. But they acquire *skill* primarily through *doing,* by bringing motor activities into the process. Thus you must really approach skill training through a series of three separate and distinct steps:

1. Gather and organize the needed knowledge.
2. Introduce the skill.
3. Allow enough time and appropriate conditions for *practice*.

Nobody really *owns* a skill until it can be performed without conscious thought. When babies learn to walk, they probably have to think about moving one foot at a time, at least for a while. But before long they go through the drill automatically; the responses are taken over at a lower level of consciousness, so that absolutely no conscious thought is involved.

In the case of other, less familiar skills, the parallel may not be quite so apparent, but it is there. *A skill is not fully developed until the person who uses it can employ it with no conscious thought or effort.*

We emphasize this fact at the risk of belaboring the point. We willingly take the risk, because, basic as the idea is, many meeting leaders frequently forget or overlook it. Even if they don't, in practice they often appear to do so. Why? Because when a meeting threatens to run overtime, what is it that almost always gets cut out? *Drill time.* When something has to give, it is the "do this over and over until you get it right" that is scissored from the agenda.

Doubtless, you've attended meetings when a new product, a new system, or a new procedure was introduced, and—*zap*—once this was done, the meeting ended abruptly. With virtually no warning, you—and everyone there with you—were left to your own devices. Unaided, you had to figure out how to put the new product or system or procedure into action, often without having more than a faint idea of how it was supposed to work.

Some organizations carry this misguided omission to even worse extremes, and thus compound their felony. At some later date they call back all the persons who attended the initial training (?) meeting and raise hell because there has been no uniform application of the new procedure. By heaping this crowning indignity upon the heads of the innocent participants, they fool themselves into believing they are "straightening out the situation." If you've ever had this happen to you—and sad to say, most of us have—you know full well that the damage thus done is often irreparable.

But there are other sins of omission and commission that are almost as bad. A poorly planned follow-up, for example, may be called in an effort to straighten out a poorly planned initial meeting. The first should never have been allowed to happen; the second just makes things worse. This misguided approach is what gives meetings a bad name.

Moral: If meetings are so poorly planned and poorly conducted that they fail to accomplish their intended purpose(s), all the apologies, cover-ups, and follow-ups in the world won't help. The important point to remember is that *all of these problems can be avoided by doing things right the first time.*

"Doing things right" means planning in advance for maximum participation, preferably with "hands-on" exercises in applying the new skill. Further, it means putting the new skill into a fun-to-learn context—and, above all—allowing the participants time to practice the skill they are expected to acquire as a result of attending your meeting.

The meeting to inspire. Please note that we say "inspire," not "motivate." (We use "inspire" in the sense of "to stimulate or impel to some creative or effective effort." The term "motivate" is more specialized, and to us means "to supply a motive for.")

We realize that some meeting leaders use the terms more or less interchangeably. We strive to differentiate, even though the terms are obviously related, and one may lead to the other.

Our view is that your meeting will "inspire" if it makes the participants feel good and want to improve their performance—as a result of seeing or hearing certain types of presentations, stories, or actions that describe ways of achieving success. We further believe that when the material is presented in the form of lively, firsthand, real-life examples, the overall effectiveness will be much increased.

People *can* be inspired to make changes in their lives—not just in their personal lives, but in their business or professional lives, as well. Sometimes, the degree of planning and dedication shown by the meeting leader can make a world of difference. We have found that the best leaders seem to have a special way of drawing a tight, clearcut relationship between past successes and the hope and expectation of future ones. It's not always easy to do, but it *can* be done. And we know, from years of observation, that any leader or presenter who has mastered the skill of presenting material in this form is bound to succeed.

The meeting to solve problems. Problem solving and conflict resolution are not one and the same. Often the two are used simultaneously or, in some instances, interchangeably. For the purposes of this book, we are addressing them separately. Using our definition of the word "problem" will most likely lead to a similar conclusion by readers:

> A problem is a situation or condition that has reached threatening proportions. People, organizational growth, or the organization's mission may be jeopardized if the condition or situation is not changed or its effects lessened.

Internal conflict can be one such problem, but certainly not the only one encountered by an organization (but we have singled out that problem for further discussion following problem solving).

Problem solving as a science is much too broad to cover within the confines of a single book, especially this one. In the *Journal of Creative Behavior* (Spring issue of 1968) an article entitled "The People, the Problems, and the Problem Solving Methods," by J. H. McPherson, set forth a list of the *sixteen* best-known problem-solving methods. All sixteen were tried, workable, and in use at that time. That was the period when there was a great proliferation of companies and individuals jumping on the bandwagon. That growth of the science or art has its benefit. Some truly great problem analysis and resolution techniques have been developed. But, let me add another dimension to the proliferation of these methods.

One of the sixteen problem-solving procedures listed was Kepner-Tregoe's method. It deserved its place, since it's one of the better ones. But during a recent six-month period, I was contacted by five different organizations that sponsored courses similar to the Kepner-Tregoe method (by their own admission), but varied in one or more of the steps. When you consider that the adding-on by latecomers is taking place on everyone else's system, you can get a more accurate estimate of the number of methods in existence.

Not only are there a good number of systems around for solving problems, but strange as it seems, most of them work—given a certain type of problem and a favorable organizational climate for employment of the specific method. That's important! If the method doesn't fit the organization's management style, you have two strikes against you before you come up to bat!

In spite of the number of systems, there is a certain commonality of steps involved in most problem-solving methods. At the risk of offending all of the dedicated people who have spent their lives furthering one system or another, let me list those steps:

1. Recognizing there is a problem

2. Determining the outcome if nothing is done

3. Defining the dimensions of the problem

4. Determining the root causes of the problem

5. Seeking tentative solutions to the problem

6. Weighing the consequences of the tentative solutions

7. Identifying the best all-around solution

8. Testing the selected solution

9. Implementing change to employ the solution

If this simplified format of problem solving is to be used, everyone who could contribute to the solution is a likely candidate to attend the meeting. In situations where the sheer number of people involved would prohibit that, a representative sample of people can be formed into a task force as spokespersons and problem solvers for the larger group. Complex problems may require a series of meetings. Indeed, some organizations have had certain problems under study for a number of *years*.

Of course, any of the steps in the procedure can be repeated as necessary. Also, No. 9 on the previous list can be the topic for one additional or even a series of meetings.

Implementing changes as a solution to a problem can take many forms, as can problem solving itself. But once again, permit me to offer some common and simplified steps:

1. The problem is defined for the audience.

2. The probable consequences are listed.

3. Audience emotions are aroused.

4. Hope is given.

5. The solution is offered.

6. The audience is told how the solution can work (preferably in their favor).

7. A commitment is gained.

8. The details are given.

9. A plan of action is outlined.

10. The audience is given the charge of implementing its portion of the plan.

If you saw some historically political overtones in the procedure for implementing change, good for you. Think about it. While you're thinking, consider how many times you've personally seen evidence that it works. After all, isn't statesmanship just another word for salesmanship?

The meeting to resolve conflict. First, some defining of the topic.

> Conflict is the clashing together or disharmonious meshing of perceptions, methods, and goals. Its roots are often in misperceptions and mistrust. Conflict resolution for the purposes of this text becomes the act of resolving, reducing, or lessening conflict to manageable proportions.

We will never be free of conflict. We live in a world filled with conflict. Some touches us individually; some permeates entire groups. When conflict reaches an uncomfortable level and is between interdependent parties, it has to be dealt with.

A common form of conflict is internal, or work related. This is the only type we'll deal with here—for example, in an integrated company, field salespeople versus internal marketing managers. To the salespeople, "the marketing managers sit in an ivory tower and deal in abstract numbers, not plans that are workable in the 'real world.'" On the other hand, marketing managers wonder among themselves why they, with all their brilliantly conceived plans, need those troublemakers in the field anyway.

Yet, there are occasions when these two factions get together to gang up on the manufacturing department for not being able to produce enough product within specs to fit every situation. On the other hand, the people in manufacturing know that they could do better if the marketing managers could accurately execute a simple marketing plan. And, if the sales force would get off their collective butts, an expanded manufacturing facility could be easily affordable.

In a competitive company, this becomes fairly commonplace, and is practiced to the degree that the organization permits. It can reach unmanageable proportions; workers become more concerned with winning the game than in mutual progress.

The reverse is the key to internal conflict resolution—clearly instilling the idea and practice of everyone winning together. This, then, replaces the notion that for every winner there has to be a loser—even within one's own organization. The work is successful when the general opinion becomes that it's easier to have all winners in an organization rather than some winners and some losers.

Actions and techniques to resolve conflict vary by the number of people involved in the conflict. The end objective is the same, resolve or reduce conflict as an impediment to reaching organizational goals. A classical format would follow these lines:

1. Reveal previously unknown information that will change or enhance each side's image of the other.
2. Let each faction give and get feedback about the others.
3. Create a group awareness of each side's current situation.
4. Evoke empathy for each other's situation.
5. Illustrate how winning together becomes easy.
6. Dispel the idea that for every winner there must be a loser.
7. Install a new mutually agreed-upon set of rules of resolving common problems and the resultant conflicts.
8. Make a charge to the organization to act as a whole against a mutual challenge or toward a group goal.

Admittedly, a bit simplified. The entire process may take a series of meetings and the assistance of skilled consultants. With them, the various milestones would be reached through the use of business or psychological games, exercises, and controlled dialogue.

Control of such meetings requires skill and experience for the best results. In this particular instance, we strongly suggest that you investigate the use of an outside consultant. If you choose to make such an investigation, the first step is identifying one of the consultants who could help. Four sources of referrals are:

- American Society for Training and Development. There is currently a referral service at their national headquarters. From this service, you can request a list of conceivable consultants for this or other topics. Contact them by calling or writing:
  American Society for Training and Development
  MIS Service
  600 Maryland Avenue, S.W., Suite 305
  Washington, D.C. 20024
- *The Buyers Guide and Consultant Directory* is also available from ASTD.
- The organizational behavior department in the school of business at a large university
- The industrial psychology department in the school of psychology at a large university
- And, last but not least, are the personal referrals from other organizations that have employed consultants for the same purpose.

We heartily recommend that you review these resources and any others at your disposal before embarking on this type of meeting planning. Putting conflict problems in the hands of an inexperienced person or your trust in an untried system can be worse than doing nothing. But, on the other hand, heavy conflict between interdependent parties needs to be resolved—and well—for the organization to reach its goals. With that said, we think our best move is to offer you the criteria we would use in selecting a consultant or consulting group:

- What system or approach do they use?
- How was the system devised, and why?
- How was it tested?
- Where has it been used?
- What successes can be attributed to the system? To the individuals employing it?
- What (if they'll tell you) were their failures?
- What is the similarity between their successes and failures and your current situation?

In the end, the determining factor has to be your opinion of the chances for success in your organization today.

Peer Rub-off

Now we'd like to return to the subject of meetings in general, and one of the built-in "fringe benefits" that almost automatically accompanies any such gatherings. We call it "peer rub-off," for lack of a better term, and it refers to the way meeting attendees learn from one another as well as from the meeting leader.

If you plan your meeting in such a way that the attendees are encouraged to participate, much valuable learning takes place in the meeting room as the participants exchange ideas.

Some of the most important and effective learning occurs during *breaks* in the meeting. Experienced meeting leaders know that the essence of "peer rub-off" is frequently achieved during the informal talk and discussion, when the attendees mutually decide how they can put into practice the ideas they have heard.

After having listened to the formal "pitch" together, they next talk among themselves and "try ideas on for size." It is instructive and exciting for a leader to stand by and watch those ideas spread, burgeon, and blossom.

A typical exchange between two salespersons talking informally during a break might go something like this:

JANE DOE: That was a pretty good idea Mr. Meeting Leader had about how to sell these new widgets, but it won't work in my sales area.
JOE BLOW: Why's that?
JANE DOE: Well, he said that *every* hardware store would fall all over itself if we followed his simple sales plan.
JOE BLOW: So?

JANE DOE: So the problem is that I don't have more than a half dozen hardware stores in my entire sales area. I sell mainly to supermarkets and small department stores.

JOE BLOW: I can see that will be a problem for you. Fact is, now that you've put it into words, I can see that your problem at least partially applies to me, too. I don't have the same mix you do, but I don't have all that many hardware stores either.

JANE DOE: Maybe we can get together during the next break and work on an angle for adapting the approach to supermarkets.

JOE BLOW: We can sure give it a try.

JANE DOE: See you then.

Somehow, it is next to impossible to get such useful and personal exchanges and interactions going by any other means—and certainly not through a mailed-out bulletin that simply announces to the sales force that some new widgets are being introduced to the market.

When the exchange of ideas ends, chances are that the participants will emerge with ways of putting the program into a context that will work for *them*. You, as the meeting leader, can feel confident that something good is going to happen. Best of all, you will know (and if you play your cards right, the participants will also know) that *you* are the person who has put the wheels in motion.

That's satisfaction!

Chapter 2

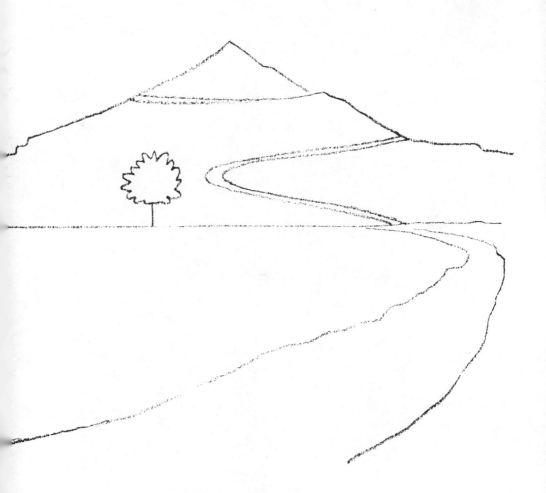

Choosing the Room and the Site

Where in this small-talking world can I find
A longitude with no platitude?

— CHRISTOPHER FRY

Factors that Can Make or Break Your Meeting

It's easy to take some things too much for granted. (Experienced meeting planners who have learned things the hard way know this entirely too well.)

Choosing the site—and the room—for a meeting might seem at first glance to be a cut-and-dried proposition.

It isn't.

Choosing the *right* combination can virtually ensure that your meeting is on the way to becoming a super-success. Choosing the *wrong* one can lead to anything from a minor disruption to a major disaster. We know a few cases in which an unfortunate choice led to a total wipe-out before the meeting even got started. (We'll give you a case history in a moment.)

The size of the meeting room, the number of square feet per person, and the number of attendees must be considered. But before you can consider any of these factors intelligently, you must decide two things: *what you want to accomplish, and what techniques you intend to use to bring that accomplishment about.*

As a general rule, participative audiences need more space than do nonparticipative ones. The higher the degree of participation, the more space needed for the audience. Similarly, the more audiovisual equipment and training aids used, the more space needed for the speaker or presenter.

Any room or any site that doesn't harmonize with and enhance the purposes of the meeting can detract (or distract) from success. And sometimes that's putting it mildly.

Case History of a Poor Site Choice

Here's an example of what we're talking about:

A company we'll call X Corporation (for obvious reasons) once scheduled a "belt-tightening" announcement meeting for their salespeople at—would you believe—a plush country club. You can imagine the joyous anticipation when the word went out that the meeting would be held in this luxurious, almost fantasylike environment.

But when the participants arrived on the premises, the first word they received was that they would not be permitted to play golf or tennis or use the other recreational facilities while they were there.

To make matters worse, the chief message of the meeting was that salespeople would be required to cut their expenses drastically in the future. No more golf dates with customers. No more unlimited expense accounts. No more picking up tabs for elaborate dinners or big-name nightclub entertainment.

This three-day "chewing out" took place in a magnificently furnished conference room with floor-to-ceiling windows offering a perfect view of the 18th green.

Compared to the company executive who planned the meeting, Captain Bligh would have won a popularity contest. When top management asked him why he chose that particular site and room, he answered, "It's close to home and the food is good." This imbecile ignored the ancient proverb, "Always put brain in gear before running mouth." Even worse, he blatantly ignored one of the basic tenets of the land of the free and the home of the brave—the one about avoiding "cruel and unusual punishment."

There were too many blunders associated with this meeting to recount them all. But—just for starters—any meeting held at an expensive and luxurious country club will inevitably be construed as "conspicuous consumption." How serious could any reasonable person be about attending a belt-tightening meeting conducted in such an atmosphere? The meeting planner is lucky he didn't find himself looking for a new job. But at least he knows now that the site and the room can play a great part in a meeting's success—or its failure.

Determining the Type of Meeting

If you're going to find the ideal room—and the ideal site—you must first know exactly what type of meeting you are going to conduct, and how much audience participation you expect.

The reason? Different types of meetings require different seating arrangements, some of which require a large number of square feet for each participant. Other considerations also play an important role. For example:

- Do the participants need writing space?
- Will it be necessary to have room to regroup people and chairs?
- How much room is needed for special equipment, training aids, and so on?

We'll suggest various seating arrangements in the next chapter, along with a discussion of basic considerations on what space is required for each, and how the various setups contribute to participation.

After you've determined what type of meeting and what kind(s) of audiovisual equipment to use, you can make a much wiser choice in finding a room that fits all needs. (Later in this chapter, we'll provide you with a checklist for rating rooms. All you'll have to do is fill in the answers and add up the score.)

Control the Environment and Control the Meeting

Meeting rooms that are cramped, hot, poorly ventilated, or dimly lighted wear participants down in a hurry. Nerves fray, tempers get short, and listening ability and retention both take nose dives.

The best rooms are those in which there is adequate space and you can control the ambiance: lighting, cooling/heating, sound, and furniture arrangement.

Adequate lighting for all purposes covers a wide range of illumination. Almost no light at all is required for showing motion pictures or slides. Medium-low lighting is best for overhead cells (transparencies). More light is required for effective note-taking. And a high concentration of light is necessary for reading.

If you plan to employ more than one of these forms of visual communication, try to procure a room that has rheostatic controls or supplementary light sources. Also, if there is a lot of window space, make sure shutters or curtains are provided to control the outside light.

How about the heating and cooling setup of the room? What kind of controls are provided? More important, can you get to them?

Sound? Consider this subject from two angles—keeping out *unwanted* sound, and distributing *wanted* sound so that the participants can hear clearly what is being said, regardless of where they are seated. Are the acoustics of the room crisp? Or does the place sound like an echo chamber? Are there any "dead spots"?

With these basics in mind, we suggest you take a look at the checklist that follows. Jim has used it successfully for years, and both of us are sure you'll find it—or your own adaptation of it—a useful tool in selecting the right room for your next meeting.

Figure 2-1. Checklist for meeting room.

1. Room is of adequate size* _____
2. Room lends itself to group meeting (no irregularities of design) _____
3. Tables/chairs can be grouped into required seating arrangement* _____

(*If you answered "no" to any of the above items, you'd better look at another room. Otherwise, continue . . .*)

4. All environmental controls for the room are easily accessible _____
5. There is a stage or platform
    Adequate size _____ Curtains _____ Other _____
6. Technical
    Proper ventilation/air conditioning _____
    Positive shut-off for telephone and intercom _____
    Room lights adequate for writing _____
    Lights on rheostat _____
    Adequate electrical outlets:
        One for each piece of equipment _____
        Correct voltage _____
        In suitable location _____
    Separate controls for separate lights _____
    Spotlights, if needed _____
    Lecterns, if needed:
        Right style _____ Reading light on lectern _____
        Sound controls on lectern _____ Light controls on lectern _____
        Right height or adjustable _____
    Acoustics _____

Sound amplifying system _____
7. Room walls
   Solid _____   Retractable _____
   Windows (What do they look out on?) _____
8. Is room adjacent to outside noise sources, such as
   Other meeting rooms _____   Kitchen _____
   Bar _____   Lobby _____
   Swimming _____   Laundry room _____
9. Will there be other meetings in the hotel at the same time? _____
   Who? _____

*See Chapter 3 for space requirements for various seating arrangements.

Refreshment and Restroom Breaks

The mind can absorb only what the rear end can endure, as the old saying goes. Let's face it, you can't get your message across to a fidgety audience. That means you must allow for frequent breaks, good restroom facilities, and well-prepared refreshments.

Many meeting leaders think of breaks only as time lost from the program, and dole them out as cautiously as a miser does with krugerrands. They are wrong— dead wrong. It is simple common sense to give breaks. When major milestones are reached, a pause in the program allows the material to sink in.

Psychologically speaking, participants best remember the first and last messages they hear in a given segment; thus, points made just before a rest break in the program are actually getting a special emphasis. Take advantage of this. If there are one or two key points that participants need to remember above all else—transmit them *right before the break.*

What happens *during* the break is important, too. Make sure to head off major distractions or inconveniences, no matter how minor they might seem to be at first glance. For example, if you call a coffee break and the coffee hasn't arrived or isn't hot, an upbeat situation can quickly turn down. Or if your group is heading for the restrooms at the same moment another larger group from across the hall is racing them to the facilities, the situation can grow uncomfortable in more ways than one. A few precautions in planning can help both situations.

Refreshments. You may naively believe that if you have specified on your agreement sheet with the hotel a refreshment break at 10 A.M., that's a guarantee you'll get it at that time. That's kind of like thinking a stop sign is going to make a New York City cabdriver come to a screeching halt. Wise meeting planners and wary pedestrians both know better.

To cut the odds closer to even money, impress upon the catering manager how fussy you are about having refreshments arrive on time, properly prepared.

That's just step one. On the morning of the meeting, stop by the catering office and ask to be introduced to the person who will be delivering the refreshments. Gently but firmly reiterate to everyone present (and especially to the actual server) the time you expect the refreshments to be served. If possible, check their order sheet to ensure that the information they have specifies exactly what you ordered—amounts and types of refreshments, cups, hot water for tea, and so on.

Sometimes, in spite of your best-laid plans, you have to change the break times after the program is under way. You'll need to act fast. Get in touch with the waiter or waitress right away. If you can't give at least thirty minutes notice, you might as well forget it. You'll almost certainly get the refreshments at the time you *originally* wanted them—regardless of how that may mess up your revised plans.

Another caution: make sure that the refreshments, when served, are easily accessible to your people, but not too accessible to other groups! In tight settings, we have found some confusion over which urn belongs to what group. We suggest you place some simple placards on the serving table to lead the groups to the proper refreshments.

Restroom facilities. Long lines or cluttered restrooms are not minor complaints—they can seriously detract from the overall effect of an otherwise excellent meeting. When you first inspect a new site, be sure to make a quick visual check of the restrooms, right along with the other facilities. Often you can spot clues of possible impending problems.

Years ago, Jim had a friend whose duties often involved checking out new eating facilities for his organization. He always made the restroom his first stop. If he found it was dirty, he would leave the restaurant without being seated. When Jim asked why, he said: "The cleanliness of the restrooms is a good indicator of their housekeeping. It's an amazingly good clue to what goes on in the kitchen. Good housekeepers keep *everything* clean—poor ones don't. It's that simple."

Says Jim: "For a long time I thought what he said might be going a bit far. But as the years go by, his message gets more firmly imprinted in my mind. Recently, I walked into a dirty restroom after having enjoyed a delicious meal—and suddenly everything went a bit sour. In my mind I was asking, 'If I had seen this first, would I have eaten here? And would I come here again?' It didn't take much thought before I answered 'no' to both questions."

It's a good bet that if restrooms look tacky during a site inspection trip, they'll probably look that way during your meeting. Of course, you could have the management clean them up—but now that you've read about Jim's friend, wouldn't you be wondering about the kitchen during each meal?

Long lines, of course, have to do with numbers of people, pieces of plumbing, and locations. When you do your "people count," count all the groups gathered at the facility, not just the number in your individual group. Here are some published standards to fit the code for the City of Houston. Codes in other cities will doubtless vary, but this will give you a good frame of reference about what's adequate. Please keep in mind, however, that these are *minimum* requirements.

Of course, proximity of the restrooms to the meeting room is important. The best is not too close but not too far. (That's what Jeff describes as one of my occasional leaps from straightforward bluntness to total ambiguity.) Here's what I mean by too close. If one of the restrooms and the meeting room share a common

TYPE OF BUILDING	WATER CLOSETS			URINALS		LAVATORIES	
	NO. OF PERSONS	NO. OF FIXTURES		NO. OF PERSONS	NU. OF FIXTURES	NO. OF PERSONS	NO. OF FIXTURES
		M	F		MALE		
THEATERS AND AUDITORIUMS	1-100	2	2	1-200	2	1-200	1
	101-200	3	3	201-400	3	201-400	2
	201-400	4	4	401-600	4	401-750	3
	OVER 400, ADD 1 FIXTURE FOR EACH ADDITIONAL 500 MALES AND ONE FOR EACH 300 FEMALES			OVER 600, ADD 1 FOR EACH ADDITIONAL 300 MALES		OVER 750, ADD 1 FOR EACH ADDITIONAL 500 PERSONS	
RESTAURANTS, CLUBS, AND LOUNGES	1-50	1	1	1-150	1	1-150	1
	51-150	2	2			151-200	2
	151-300	3	4			201-400	3
	OVER 300, ADD 1 FIXTURE FOR EACH ADDITIONAL 200 PERSONS			OVER 150, ADD 1 FIXTURE FOR EACH ADDITIONAL 150 MALES		OVER 400, ADD 1 FIXTURE FOR EACH ADDITIONAL 150 PERSONS	

Figure 2-2. Minimum facilities based upon occupant load, City of Houston.

separating wall, that can be too close. Plumbing noises have a way of echoing along and through thin walls, especially if there are problem valves in the line. Too far is when the restrooms are on the "back forty," and you're plowing through a meeting at the front corner of the complex.

I (Jim) am reminded of a meeting I recently worked on in a very nice conference center adjacent to a major hotel. The single meeting room on the top floor of the center would accommodate about 2000 persons when it was totally open. By means of roller curtains, it could be subdivided into four rooms, each accommodating 500 persons or more. The building designer had the restroom facilities well isolated from the meeting room, and there were more than enough fixtures. The problem was that *they were all in one room*. (Well, not quite! I should have said, one room each for *men* and *women*.)

If you drew meeting room No. 4, the walk was almost two city blocks long. So, every break you started walking, because if you didn't have a sense of urgency when you left the meeting room, you would have acquired it by the time you reached the restroom. There were, nevertheless, some good points. The restroom was one of the largest I've ever seen. It was spotlessly clean — you could go snow-blind just looking at the endless rows of gleaming white porcelain. Poor location excluded, it did meet the other criteria a meeting planner should always look for: sound isolation and enough fixtures to accommodate the guests.

Outdoor facilities. The most ridiculous placing of restroom facilities I've ever encountered was at a huge outdoor festival; the occasion was a well-known country singer's concert, birthday, and Fourth-of-July party, all rolled into one. The event, which was to run for two days, was held in the Texas hill country on a 200-acre "spread."

One of the features in their advertising was that there would be 1500 outdoor toilets. There were. The problem was that they were all lined up in one spot — 1500 porta-potties cheek-to-cheek (so to speak) and about a mile from the closest parking space.

Now you know most of our pet peeves, but here's one more — "cuteness" in restroom signs. You've seen them: Pointers and Setters; Braves and Squaws; Messrs. and Mesdames; Lords and Ladies; and so on, ad nauseam. The most baffling (at least temporarily) such combination is one that Jim saw recently. It looked like this:

Figure 2-3.
Signs on restroom doors.

To get a jump on the crowd, Jim was the first one out of the theater for intermission. By the time he had figured out that the sign on the left was a hair ribbon and the one on the right was a mustache, he found himself waiting far back in the line!

So, one more tip. If you are at a facility that goes for cuteness or if the restrooms are obscured by potted plants, twisting hallways, or the like, *make sure to give the participants specific directions.* For example, "The ladies' room is down the hall to the left and the men's room down the hall to the right; coffee is on the mezzanine; and we'll reconvene here in fifteen minutes."

Choosing the Best Seating Arrangement

Let there be spaces in your Togetherness.
— KAHLIL GIBRAN

How Much Involvement?

Meeting participants get the message best when the leader encourages them to get into the act. The deeper they become involved, the deeper the message penetrates.

Most good leaders learn many techniques to make sure that the participants really *participate*. We'll discuss some of these later. For now, suffice it to say that participation can be done in a group, on a team, or as an individual. It can be as simple as a show of hands, or as complex as an intensive practice of individual skills, one on one.

There's a lot of middle ground, too. Group exercises, question-and-answer sessions, quizzes, and teamwork are some representative ways of getting a group to participate.

Very early in your planning, you must consider carefully how much involvement or participation is desirable, and with whom. Although you are the meeting leader, you may not have all the answers. Or, perhaps you don't want to be solely responsible for making the decision. Maybe you'll even want to give the participants a voice in choosing. They may have important considerations—at least in their own minds. (Sometimes the best leaders do the least obvious leading. Their art may lie in getting the message across by making it easy and natural for the participants to learn from one another.)

By now you may be wondering what all this has to do with seating arrangements. The answer is—*everything!* If, for example, your message is intended simply to convey information, you can use a room with theater-type seating, with chairs in rows fairly close together. But if you are teaching, say, a new job or a new phase of an old one, you will need to teach *skill* as well as knowledge.

The knowledge of how it's to be done can be transmitted by any effective means of communication. *Skill* is a different story; it requires putting the knowledge into action. That takes practice. And that takes room. Room to write, or build, or assemble, or whatever other manual needs the skill calls for.

You, as the leader, are the best judge of how much depth of participation is needed to make your message (and your meeting) most effective. That decision, in turn, will dictate (at least in part) the seating arrangements best adapted to your aims.

Here are some of the classical patterns for group meetings. Alongside each we've included an explanation of the space required.

Theater Style

For minimum group involvement, arrange your seats in theater style, with the entire audience facing the speaker or screen.

Figure 3-1. Theater style. Allow about 6 square feet per person exclusive of aisles, speaker's space, and room for equipment.

Schoolroom Style

For medium group involvement, set up the seats in schoolroom style, with each person having a writing surface or a small desk. The desk is used for reading, writing, note-taking, and so forth. The main discussion is back and forth between the meeting leader and the group at large, or between the instructor and individuals in the group.

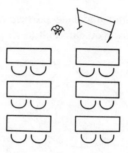

Figure 3-2. Schoolroom style. Allow approximately 10 square feet per person in addition to space for aisles, the speaker, and equipment.

The "Senate" and "Herringbone" Patterns

Some variations are the "Senate" fashion, for rooms with built-in multi-level floors; or the "herringbone" pattern, for rooms with a single level of floor. In both arrangements, the main focal points are the instructional surface, writing board, screen or chart table, and the meeting leader.

Figure 3-3. Senate style. Allow at least 15 square feet per person in addition to aisles and stage or pit.

The herringbone pattern can be especially effective for the meeting leader who likes to walk and talk at the same time, or for the leader who wants to get close to certain members of the audience during certain points of the delivery.

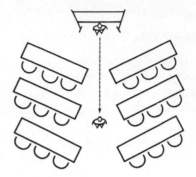

Figure 3-4. Herringbone style. Allow about 10 to 12 square feet per person plus an extra-wide aisle down the center.

Conference Style

For maximum audience participation, a conference-style setup is excellent for small groups. You can do it in either of the following ways:

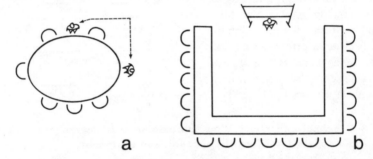

Figure 3-5. Conference styles. (*a*) The amount of space required here is dictated by the size of the table and is inflexible; (*b*) this is the most costly in space of any of the room setups.

This should not be considered for more than twenty-four participants. The problem is that in order to form the "U," people are physically pushed apart. In spite of its space requirements, however, this is an effective method for involvement among participants. The leader can interject, stimulate, or withdraw from the discussions.

In the first of the two small conference setups, you'll note that we gave two seating options for the meeting leader. If the discussion is to be mainly between participants, the leader could choose the *end seat*. However, if the leader wants to maintain full control, whether orally or silently, the seat at the *side* would be the preferred choice.

Making a side seat (preferably the one in the exact center, facing the door) the seat of power may be contradictory to everything you've learned in the past. So be it. All we can say is, in the vernacular of the street, "Don't knock it until you've tried it." It works.

"Buzz Groups"

"Buzz groups" are excellent for maximum participation for large groups. The name comes from the noise given off by the groups or teams at work. In this method, the speaker poses situations or hands out case histories. Then the table team members work on the problem, either individually or in concert.

At the end of their work period, they report their findings or answers to the team member they've elected secretary or spokesperson, who, in turn, reports to the room at large. The meeting leader then records findings on the chalkboard and acts as moderator.

The real action, though, is in the ideas exchanged between team members as they prepare their spokesperson to make the team report. Further learning action occurs when team members get into the spirit of competition with other teams.

A variation of the buzz group theme is to get people in any one of the other seating arrangements for portions of a meeting. Then, from time to time, the teams withdraw to separate corners of the room (or to separate rooms) for team-work assignments.

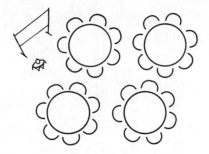

Figure 3-6. Buzz group style. Allow approximately 10 square feet per person plus space needed for equipment and for the speaker.

Now—
Find That "Ideal Room"

*Many eyes go through the meadow, but few see the
flowers in it.*

— RALPH WALDO EMERSON

Keep a Constant Lookout

With your space requirements and desired room setup firmly in mind, your next
job is to find the ideal room—one that is the right size, one in which you can
control the environment, and, of course, one in a setting that enhances what
you're doing in the meeting room.

Always remember—*good meeting rooms are where you find them.*

Think how much better the belt-tightening meeting could have been if the planner had scheduled the boardroom of a neighborhood bank for it. He could have
added to the atmosphere by starting the meeting with, "This meeting is about
saving money. What better place to talk about it than in the boardroom of our
local depository for company funds?"

You may not have thought about it before, but meeting rooms in banks, savings
and loan firms, and similar organizations, are available for your use. Call your
bank and ask them if they have such a room. If they don't, ask them what bank
might. Or, try calling a couple on your own. You'll be pleasantly surprised at the
number of rooms available.

We urge you to *get this information now,* even if you don't have an immediate
use for a bank's meeting room. File the information away for future use—the time
will come when you'll need to consider using such a room. And having the possibilities already lined up beats the daylights out of conducting a frantic last-minute
search.

While we're on the subject, now is a good time to make a point about filing
away information for future use. Any time you visit hotels, motels, or conference
centers, check out the meeting rooms. See what's available, note your impressions, and file the notes away. If you have a camera with you, take a picture or
two to jog your memory at a later date when memory has grown hazy.

Some Alternatives You May Not Have Considered

As we have said, good meeting rooms are where you find them. You'd be surprised at some of the strange and seemingly unlikely places we've found them.
The important thing was that, at the time they were needed, they filled the bill
for location, convenience, or general atmosphere. Here are a few examples of
some different types of places where we've found meeting space.

- Department stores
- Suites of shopping center's management companies
- Auditoriums in private schools
- Lodges and other fraternal organizations
- Veteran organizations
- Large restaurants

One thing that all the last three have in common is that their main usage is during the evening hours. During the day they are often unused—therefore, available. But be sure to check possible problems in advance. Because you would be using the rooms during the day when janitorial service is usually scheduled, you might have to cut off your meeting by 3 or 4 P.M. to allow time for the rooms to be made ready for evening use. You might even have to arrange special room-cleaning services and that could be a bit of a hassle. But if everything else is right, the hassle involved is well worth it.

When we were comparing notes on unusual room arrangements, Jim recalled one that had turned out to be a real winner—but one that he had almost entirely overlooked. It was in a building owned by a city park department. Not only was the room well laid-out and functional, but it was in the center of an arboretum. This formed an excellent sound barrier that effectively filtered out almost all outside noise.

Remember—it doesn't hurt to ask!

Don't Stop Looking Too Soon

Although meeting rooms are where you find them, don't settle for the first one you inspect. Choose only the one that is right for your meeting. That is the subject of our next discussion. But before we leave this one, a few more tips on choosing an overall location are in order.

Hotels and motels are usually, but not always, the prime suppliers of meeting rooms. In fact, that's an important part of their business. The problem with this is that sometimes meeting planners forget they are engaged in a buyer/seller transaction. As a result, unwary meeting planners can come out with a little (or even a lot) less than they could have bargained for.

By this, we don't mean you should enter a negotiation with the thought of "beating someone out of something" or making a one-sided deal. What we do mean is to keep your cool, show a little detachment, and use your common sense. Look things over critically, sample the food (if any is to be served), and thoroughly discuss all aspects of the financial arrangements.

Hotels and motels usually have sales brochures containing schematic drawings or floor plans of their meeting rooms. Most of these drawings are to exact scale, but once in a while you'll find that a particular artist used a "rubber ruler." Maybe those three small black dots shown in the drawing are columns, six feet in diameter, planted right in front of the lectern.

The best way to make sure you won't wind up dissatisfied—or worse—is to look things over for yourself, well in advance of the meeting. If you have to go to a strange city to conduct a meeting and it's impractical for you to check things out for yourself, get a *trusted* acquaintance to do it for you.

Food Service—Getting the Most for Your Money

"The proof of the pudding is in the (a) eating (b) tasting (c) quality (d) cost (e) all of the above (f) none of the above." Choose your own answer or answers, but check them all out any time you're dealing with food that is served banquet-style. The pictures in the catering department's brochure are always pretty, but only by taste can you tell if the chicken is like molded rubber!

When you're checking out a hotel's food, keep in mind that the banquet food is not their regular fare—and may not even be prepared in the regular kitchen. Banquet or catered meals are usually closely portion-controlled, convenient to prepare, and easy to serve. That's the hotel's side of it. From your side, you're going to pay more per serving than you would for regular dining-room food. There are a couple of reasons for this: (1) the cost for renting the room may be included in the meal cost; and (2) it takes extra work on the part of the kitchen help and staff to prepare and serve.

We're not saying that you shouldn't order from preselected menus. We just want you to know some alternatives. For example, a small group could eat in the public dining room and order from the regular menu. Another alternative to the standard banquet fare of chicken or roast beef, new potatoes, and peas, is to order something special. Jim says it has worked well for him in the past to have the catering manager invite the head chef to one or more of the planning sessions for major meetings. Jim would simply tell the chef that he wanted something different from what was listed on the preprinted banquet menu, and suggest that the chef use some culinary imagination. The chef is usually intrigued—perhaps even inspired—by the challenge. Of course, a meeting of the minds must be reached before giving final approval. Using this technique, it is often possible to come up with some exceptionally good meals, usually at no greater cost per serving than the standard banquet prices. The approach works best when a large group is involved, but it's worth considering for the smaller ones as well.

Drink—and What You Need to Know About It

Liquor pricing practices can be important to your meeting budget. If, in fact, you regularly serve liquor at or after your meetings, knowing some of the "inside scoop" about how you're charged can save you a lot of bucks. The four most common ways of pricing liquor are by the bottle, by the drink, a per capita charge for a set period of time, or (and the hotel people may not tell you it's possible unless you bring it up) your organization furnishes the liquor and the hotel levies a corkage charge.

"By the bottle" should mean just that. How that translates is, if the seal is broken, you bought it. Some hotel bartenders have a knack of keeping at least two bottles of each variety of liquor open at each serving station at all times. So, at the end of the evening you have a full bottle of bourbon with the seal broken, and a partially empty bottle—and the same with Scotch, gin, vodka, plus partially empty bottles of all the less popular liquors—and that's from each service bar.

At the end of the party, you may as well take these with you—you bought them—and at anywhere from $18 to $50 a bottle. The exact prices depend on the brand and the hotel. These prices may sound expensive, and they are—but it still might be the most economical way to buy. The per-bottle charge includes all of the ice, mixes, stemware, and, supposedly, all the bartenders you need. We say "supposedly," because for big get-togethers, the number of bartenders needed is often underestimated by hotel personnel, resulting in poor service and long lines. *When you're making arrangements, negotiate the number of service bars and bartenders you want.*

"Per-drink" charges are just that; they cover all the extras, including the fee for the bartenders. The number of drinks that can be poured from a quart bottle depends on the hotel's policy and the bartender's skill. The range is all the way from twenty to thirty-eight. Ask the catering manager what their practice is. The difference in overall costs between this and the per-bottle charge depends on the ratio of liquor served to the amount purchased, and how "stiff" the drinks are. It will pay you to check the figures out with your handy-dandy pocket calculator.

If it's a very small meeting—say, ten persons or fewer—"by the drink" usually results in the least expensive tab. For larger groups, consider by-the-bottle charges.

"Per capita" charges are pretty much self-explanatory. A variation of this plan is that, on occasion, per capita charges include some food, too. For instance, the hotel may offer you a two-hour cocktail party and furnish all the canapés, hors d'oeuvres, and cocktails required for, say, $15 a person. To help you estimate the "per-drink" cost of this type of cocktail party, we have included a chart so you can look up the average number of drinks consumed (per person) during a given time span.

NO. OF GUESTS	½ HOUR	1 HOUR	1½ HOURS	2 HOURS
25-55	2	3½-4	4-4½	4½-5
60-104	2	3½-4	4	4½-5
105-225	2	3	4	4½-5
230-300	1½-2	2½-3	3	3½-4
315-& UP	1½-2.	2½-3	3	3½-4

BASED ON ALL MALE ATTENDANCE — EASY ACCESS TO BARS
1. WITH 50% FEMALE ATTENDANCE — REDUCE BY 25%
2. WITH 100% FEMALE ATTENDANCE — REDUCE BY 30%

Figure 4-1. Reception drink estimator. (Courtesy of Convention Sales Department, Schenley Affiliated Brands Corporation.)

"Corkage charges" are levied by hotels for serving *your* liquor to your guests. The system works something like the by-the-bottle arrangement. The difference is that you buy the liquor elsewhere, and the hotel has it served at so much per bottle. These charges usually include ice, mixes, and so on. This type of arrangement is no longer as common as it once was (when many states allowed liquor sales by the bottle, but not by the drink), but it is still practiced, so you might as well check out the possibilities.

The method you use for ordering liquor depends on the number of guests and the intended time span of the cocktail party. This, of course, is tempered by whether the group is comprised of average, less-than-average, or higher-than-average consumers. With the estimating scale and a little bit of practice, you'll be able to hit liquor needs right on the button. When you can consistently do that, you'll save anywhere from a few dollars to a real bundle on the social hours you host.

Financial Arrangements

Hotels, motels, and restaurants, like everyone else, want to make sure that they are going to get their money. Therefore, they will probably ask you (a) to fill out a financial statement of the creditworthiness of your organization, or (b) to make a substantial deposit. (Or both.)

Restaurant bills are usually, but not always, payable immediately upon completion of the event. Hotels and motels may give your organization an extended final billing to allow for checking on individual charges, especially in the case of large meetings. The practice in these instances is to make a deposit and a substantial payment on the bill at the time of the function. Final payment is then made after all charges related to your meeting have been totaled and verified for correctness.

You should try to nail down what items will be charged to your organization, and the time to do it is not at the last minute, but well in advance of the meeting. For instance, a company or organization conducting a multiday meeting may have all attendees' subsistence charges billed directly to them. Thus, each person pays his or her room and meal bills upon checking out.

In other instances, all charges may go on one master billing to the host organization. The way that works is relatively simple: each person, upon check-out, approves the amount of the room rent and other charges by signing the bill. Then, it all goes on the master account. There are variations on this theme. *Get a clear understanding with the hotel about which individual items (if any) can be charged to your organization's master billing.* When you host meetings that have banquets or dress dinners, keep in mind that some of the guests or spouses may want to make visits to beauty shops or hair stylists, rent tuxes, buy flowers, and so on, often in the hotel gift shops or other facilities. These charges—and those for long-distance phone calls, recreation or sport activities, or bar bills—can wreck a meeting budget if they show up unexpectedly on your master billing.

As a courtesy to your guests, we strongly recommend that you include with their check-in packet a letter that spells out what they can or cannot charge to a master account. To make assurance doubly sure, you might also list the procedure to be used at check-out time.

Master accounts are a necessity even when guests are paying their own way. There are still group functions, meals, coffee breaks, and cocktail parties for which one or more persons in your organization will have to sign the bill. The fewer the number of persons authorized to do this, the less the confusion at the time when all the bills must be reconciled and settled. One idea you might explore for large, multiday meetings is to assign different people to different categories. Then, one person would sign all checks or bills falling in a given category.

Whatever your financial arrangements, make sure they are clear to all persons involved. One way to correct possible misunderstandings in advance is to send a confirming letter or summary of your understanding to the hotel. Copies to key people in your organization will help get everybody on the same wave length.

Overall Arrangements

If you are considering booking a sizable meeting into a hotel, we would suggest you meet with the hotel's general manager. This is especially true if you are making the booking months in advance of the event. At a later date, you may need his or her assistance should problems arise. Also, catering managers, sales managers, and salespeople for hotels change employment fairly frequently. Accordingly, many professional meeting planners make it a standard practice to check back at intervals just to maintain their contacts.

You might show up on meeting day only to find that the lower-echelon people you have been dealing with aren't even there any more. That's why you should know the general manager. (Of course, they've been known to leave, too.)

Regardless of the size of your meeting, when you and the supplier, hotel or restaurant, reach an agreement, *put it in writing.* Which rooms, what dates, what persons to contact, all are much too important to trust to memory. Also, large meetings are booked months or even years in advance. A written reference copy assures that details can be kept fresh in your mind.

One way to cover all bases is to use a checklist. We have included here a copy of one that we use, as a sample. Jim's method in using this form is to have the responsible person at the hotel sign the form and keep a copy so that they'll both have the same information for future reference.

Figure 4-2. Group meeting—requirement summary.

Meeting place _____

Date of event _____ Duration of event _____ Arrival date_____

Sleeping accommodations _____

Meeting rooms _____ Time_____

Food or beverage

    Breakfast _____ Time _____

    Coffee break _____ Time _____

    Lunch _____ Time _____

    Coffee break _____ Time _____

    Cocktail party _____ Time _____

    Dinner _____ Time _____

Contacts
    For the company _____
    For the hotel _____
Credit arrangements _____
Check-out time _____

Complete a copy of page 2 of this form for each use of each meeting or dining room.

Audience seating _____

Room lighting _____

Head table _____   Table lectern _____

Other lecterns _____   Where _____

Extra microphones _____

Stage or platform size _____   Height _____   Location _____

Stage lighting _____

Special drapery _____

Other requirements
    Water _____   Name cards _____   Ashtrays _____

    Paper and pencils _____   Other _____

Equipment

    Projectors _____

    Screens _____

    Easels _____

    Blackboard _____

    Posted directions _____

    Other _____

Personnel

    Projectionists _____

    Porter _____

    Extra waiters _____

    Stenographer _____

    Message center _____

    Other _____

_____   _____

Hotel Representative   Company Representative

When Words
Are Not Enough

One picture is worth a thousand words.
                              —OLD CHINESE PROVERB

Words and Pictures—Thank God for Both

Old Chinese proverbs are *almost* always right, even if an hour later they leave you wondering. Indeed, we would suggest taking *any* proverb with a small dash of soy sauce. Every rule has its exception (says another proverb), even this one.

For example, we'd hate to describe a complex labor contract in terms of a single picture, chart, or photograph. Conversely, we'd have a hard time explaining an intricate geometrical design if we couldn't draw a picture of it. And we'd hate to have you visualize a camel from what we said to you about it—at least not without waving our hands in a few vigorous gestures.

The fact is, we believe pictures are great—and often indispensable. But we're hooked on words, too. Some wise observer once said that, given the choice of an ordinary picture versus a thousand words of his own choosing—say the Beatitudes, the Gettysburg Address, and a couple of Shakespeare's sonnets—he'd take the thousand words every time!

There are points on both sides. That's why the next few chapters are designed to explain some of the options you have for combining words and pictures for maximum effectiveness.

To do this, after picking the brains of many professional A/V experts, we're passing on to you the techniques they use in the real world—all practical, none theoretical. Some of these tricks are relatively new; others have been around for a long, long time.

Undoubtedly, you're already familiar with some of them. Even so, for convenience of reference, we'll remind you of them here anyway. Some of the newer ones are still esoteric enough that not all professionals have caught up with them yet; that's how fast the technology is growing and changing.

Audiovisual Aids: The Vital Ingredient of Presentations

We've seldom (correction: make that *never*) met an experienced meeting leader who would even *consider* putting on a major presentation without using one or more kinds of audiovisual aid.

Why? Good graphics are key ingredients in helping the audience grasp the ideas being presented—particularly if those ideas are at all abstract. *Visualization* is the name of the game. Most of us can understand difficult concepts much better if we are able to form a clear visual image of them in our imagination. Doing this, however, often puts quite a strain on the *unaided* imagination. Things move much faster and easier if the mind's eye gets an active boost from some well-chosen illustrations.

Increasing your own understanding. Helping your audience to visualize is just Benefit Number One. Just as important is the help that graphics can give *you*, particularly in the very early stages of putting a presentation together.

Does this sound mysterious? We'll hasten to explain: Like most professionals, we have discovered that to use graphics properly we must first visualize our upcoming presentation in our *own* imagination. And guess what—as we begin to do this, mentally twisting and turning our ideas around into forms that lend themselves to the best use of graphics, we find ourselves understanding our own ideas much better than before.

It's a fascinating process. Try it! As you begin to think in terms of helping *others* to visualize *your* ideas, you'll find yourself gaining flashes of insight you might otherwise have missed.

What happens?

We don't claim to understand the process fully, but apparently this "picturing process" enables you to wheel both halves of your brain into action at the same time. Psychologists and other experts on the learning and thinking processes tell us that the brain's two hemispheres apparently function almost independently most of the time.

One side appears to be designed for dealing with abstraction—including words, which, along with numbers, are the ultimate abstraction.

The other side appears better suited to dealing with physical senses, actions and skills, perhaps with the emotions, and thus indirectly with the creative aspects of music and art. As Pogo or another of our favorite philosophers may have said, "We don't really understand what we know about it—or maybe it's the other way around."

If the real experts on the subject want to say we've loused up the theory, we'll be the first to confess it. Maybe that's because the two hemispheres of our brains seem to work at cross-purposes a good deal of the time. We're not too sure they are even on good speaking terms; sometimes they don't appear even to speak the same language.

But our own experiences tell us that when we start thinking in terms of graphics to illustrate our words, we mysteriously seem to begin meshing *both* halves—a consummation devoutly to be wished.

And (the logic sounds credible, even if we're making it up) when your mind meshes this way, your presentation will mesh the same way. The result? The members of your audience will be carried effortlessly along with you, meshing both hemispheres of *their* brains, and understanding your most abstruse points with minimal pain and suffering.

You can test the theory. Check us out on this; we believe you'll be persuaded of the truth of our statements. Start thinking in terms of *visuals* as well as *words* even in the earliest stages of your planning. You are likely to discover that the heart of your presentation will be in the graphics. You'll be able to zero in—with amazing clarity—on the facts you depict on the charts or graphs or slides.

Of course, this doesn't *always* follow. Nothing is ever that simple. *Most* of the time, you'll be using words to stress or interpret the facts that the graphics so clearly depict. But in plenty of cases the converse may be true. Again, allowing for the fact that we love words as well as pictures, we have encountered cases in which the visuals turn out to be simply an aid to the audience's understanding of the *spoken* commentary.

Whichever way the ball bounces, you'll find a clearcut benefit: imaginative, well-planned use of audiovisuals can make all the difference between a deadly, boring presentation and one that holds the audience transfixed.

Graphics—The "Invisible" Support

Of course, we (and you, the audience) can see the graphics. At least all of us had better be able to—that, after all, is what graphics are designed for. Then how can we be so patently absurd as to describe them in the above heading as being "invisible"?

Forgive the pun, but it depends on how you look at them. The *audience* sees them just as the presenter intends for them to—as visual aids to the presentation. But the *presenter* can look at them in a twofold way that carries a built-in fringe benefit: *notes!*

Many speakers—even those priding themselves on their memory—become terrified at the prospect of facing an audience without notes. If you ever have anxiety dreams (and speakers often do), you may awaken some night in a cold sweat: you've dreamed you are making a major presentation to a roomful of VIPs and suddenly your mind draws a total blank.

Scary? You'd better believe it.

And that's where the "invisible" visual aids come in—a marvelously helpful cue to your memory in the most unobtrusive way. (After all, the audience believes you're showing all those graphics just for *their* benefit.)

Only *you* will know the real truth: that you have a handy-dandy outline reminding you point by point of what comes next. This guarantees you won't come up missing in the clutch. You won't leave out any points, and you won't put them in the wrong order. (At least you won't if you line up your slides or other aids carefully and correctly. Murphy's Law can catch any of us—if there is the slightest chance of messing them up, we're going to mess them up. We'll talk more about Murphy's Law, and how to beat it, later on.)

Foolproof Visual Aids?

Sorry, folks. There aren't any.

And that's the good news. Now for the bad news.

The fact is, *graphics can be dangerous.*

We're not just talking about the fancy or complicated ones, either. It is true that electronic and mechanical gadgets are always the scariest. But even a chalk-board can be a disaster if it hasn't been properly cleaned, or the chalk keeps breaking—or sq-u-e-e-a-a-a-k-k-k-ing—or whatever.

We've already said that well-done graphics make a good presentation better. But there is always the chance that, poorly prepared or improperly used, they can turn your show into a nightmare. Murphy's Law again. Nothing can devastate a presenter more than to have the visuals botched in any of the endless ways that sometimes happen despite the most careful preparations. We could tell you some horror stories—but we'll save them for later. There is already enough bad news here to hold you for a while.

Attention Grabber? or Distraction?

Graphics are usually designed to attract attention. What's so bad about that? Isn't that the purpose of using them?

Well, not if those graphics distract your audience from the message you're striving to put across.

How could that be?

The sad truth is that it's all too easy. As we've already said, there often appears to be built-in conflict between the two hemispheres of the brain. This conflict means, for one thing, that your audience may forget to listen to your well-chosen words, if the graphics you are using to illustrate them have a mesmerizing effect. If the visual aspect—looking—takes over, it can lead to the total exclusion of your oral message.

Sometimes that can happen if your illustrations are a smidgen too "clever," or if the colors chosen are too garish, or if other elements seem jarring or inappropriate. We can all agree that "entertainment value" is great—we'd be crazy to knock it. But strong visual impact, if it misses the target, isn't worth a plugged Swiss franc.

Did that last sentence seem strained to you? Overdone? Too much striving for effect?

That's what we intended. The device probably made you think more about it *as a device* than it made you think about the *point* we were trying to make. Let's take the comparison apart and see what went wrong. Here goes:

The obvious expression, the standard vernacular phrase, is "plugged nickel." The phrase is trite, worn out, a cliché. It is probably offensive to anyone concerned with literary style. *But*—it allows the reader's mind to stay on the *subject.* Our strained effort at finding a new twist on the old phrase, on the other hand, tends to call attention to itself. It might not be so bad except that the "change" is not appropriate. Even a plugged Swiss franc is worth decidedly more than an unplugged American nickel. We hope this apparently aimless meandering into the realm of economics has indirectly helped make our point: *illustrations should stick to the subject.*

Do Your Homework

If all this bad news makes you decide *not* to use graphics, at least you'll have much less opportunity for something to go wrong. But you wouldn't want to take the easy way out, would you?

Weigh the benefits, as well as the dangers, before you decide. If you've worked high enough up on the executive ladder to be in charge of putting on a presentation, you are bound to have guts enough to try the harder way—if it promises greater success. And that often is what good graphics can do for you. But your decision must be based on thinking the problem through—all the way. Do your homework; we'll help you by giving you a brief professional checklist of items to consider: first, some *dos,* then some *don'ts.* Here goes.

Dos

- *Do* choose the right kind of visual aid or aids. Make sure they are appropriate to the audience, the setting, the room, the subjects to be covered, and so on.

- *Do* prepare them properly. Get help if you need it.

- *Do* check them out in advance in every possible way. That includes trying them out on the actual equipment you are going to use, in the room where you're going to use them.

- *Do* rehearse, preferably before a friendly but critical group of associates who will tell you what you are doing wrong as well as what you are doing right. Rehearse—and keep rehearsing until you are sure you know exactly what you are doing and get rid of all the things you are doing wrong, or that don't add to the desired effect you are seeking.

Don'ts

- *Don't* improvise something half-baked, just because it seems easy and looks as if it *might* work.

- *Don't* use unfamiliar equipment. *Always* check it out before the show goes on. For example, if you rehearse with one kind of slide projector and do your actual show with a different kind, you are very likely to find yourself in deep trouble.

- *Don't* go on without proper rehearsal using *all* your aids and props *exactly as you intend to use them in the real act.*

- *Never* go on without having an emergency plan or fallback position in case something goes wrong.

If you ignore any of these points, you'll be sorry. But if you follow our advice faithfully, you may never find out about Murphy's Law except by hearsay.

Choosing the
Appropriate
Visual Aid(s)

Be Aware of Your Choices

Many presenters make a career of putting on the same old show and using the same old visual aids. Some of them do okay, but they are still missing a bet; many new and exciting options are open, and most of them aren't all that hard to use.

We could give pages of examples, but for practicality, let's boil the choices down to those you are likely to find most *useful, practical, readily available, and affordable.* They include:

- Models or mock-ups
- Flipcharts
- Chalkboards
- Flannelboards
- Overhead projectors
- Slide projectors

- Filmstrip projectors
- Motion picture projectors (mostly Super-8 or 16mm)
- Videotape and videodisc
- Multimedia presentations
- Other (mostly auxiliary) aids such as audio tapes, phonograph records, sound effects, lighting effects, and so on

These, then, are your most likely choices. How are you going to decide which aid, or combination of aids, to use?

Getting Down to Basics—Checklist 1A

As usual, we recommend using checklists to help make your choices. We'll give you a very basic one first:

- What is the size and make-up of the group?
- What equipment is *available?*
- What kind of room will be used (size, shape, acoustics, lighting, etc.)?
- What production sources are available to you?
- What medium or media are you most comfortable with? (You'd better not try out anything too new or fancy in a big, important presentation until after you've had a chance to get some hands-on experience in a less demanding context.)

If you can truly say you know all the answers to the questions just listed, you're at least on your way. Remember, the first purpose of your graphic aids is to help the audience visualize facts, figures, and concepts. That's why it is so important that you begin analyzing your problems systematically from the beginning. All things being equal, you are first going to start with the simplest, easiest, and cheapest solutions.

Fitting Graphics to Communication Points—Checklist 1B

This next checklist simply tacks on to the first one. Now, however, you are getting down to the nitty-gritty. Don't be superficial about answering these questions. Think them through carefully.

1. Determine the minimum number of essential points that you *must* communicate to get your message across properly. (Can you cut down or eliminate any of of these points?)

2. Determine ways you can round off figures, or make one or two words serve as captions instead of five or six. (We're getting ahead of ourselves here, and we'll explain in detail later, but a very important "rule" is to avoid putting on a single chart or slide any more material than the audience can readily grasp in about thirty seconds.)

3. Try to choose just *one* clearly depictable point for each visual. (There is one exception: If you're dealing with material that is relatively familiar to the audience, you'll be able to combine a number of points, fairly quickly, on a single visual. Even so, the amount of detail you should "pack in" this way is considerably less than most presenters would like to believe.)

4. Try to translate complex ideas or figures into a simplified form such as a pie chart or bar graph. Sometimes you'll be able to combine a few words and a simple cartoon. Occasionally, photographs, with or without captions, may be extremely effective.

5. Seek ways to relate the graphics to the spoken remarks. Think primarily in terms of *key words*.

6. Always keep in mind the need for an overall effect of consistency. Taken as a group, your visuals must be *unified*. Avoid using disparate types of lettering, widely varying artistic styles, or inconsistent formats. If you have an art department available as a support service, call in the art director (or the artist who will actually be working on the project) *early*. Don't wait until the last minute. A trained artist knows about such refinements as choosing colors, families of typefaces, and so on, that those of us who are not artists are not even aware of. The differences in impact that result from wrong choices of color or typeface can be enormous. Even laypersons will recognize that something is wrong, although they may not know why.

Enough. Although the checklists we have just given are basic and extremely important, you won't be able to use them properly without more information. You need to know what your choices are as you consider each point, and we haven't explained them to you yet. Let's rectify that situation right now.

Consider the Simple Ways First

For practicality, we'll discuss the simplest and easiest options first. Then, if they do not seem appropriate or sufficiently effective, it's time to move up to the more elaborate techniques. *Note:* Just because we suggest looking at the simple methods first does not mean that we recommend them in preference to the more sophisticated methods. Let us emphasize strongly that the more elaborate techniques are often worth the extra time, effort, and cost *if they will achieve the effects you seek.* All we are saying is, in the language of the street, "Don't use a sledgehammer to kill a roach."

The next chapter sets forth what meeting leaders often call the "nonelectronic media." We are not thrilled with the terminology, but we seem to be stuck with it. Then, in Chapter 8 we'll tell you about "electronic media." Obviously, you will have to study these chapters in tandem before you can make well-reasoned choices. We've divided the material simply as a device to make the information presented easier to follow.

When to Use
Nonelectronic Media

In speaking, writing, or presentations, set a logical pattern and then stick to it.

—JIM AND JEFF

Breaking Our Own Rule

We have long advocated the "rule" shown at the top of this page. But we also advocate breaking this rule, or any other, if there is good reason for it. We think we have one. That is why, although the first item on our list of choices in Chapter 6 is "models and mock-ups," we choose not to talk about them until the end of the chapter. Trust us!

Okay—on to the business at hand.

Anything you have to plug in or anything with moving parts can be trouble with a capital "T." That's why the old-fashioned flipcharts and chalkboards keep right on being popular. It's hard to say which of these is simpler—or easier. You could say it's a toss-up; that's another word for "flip," so let's start with flipcharts.

Flipcharts

Flipcharts are in many ways the *safest* visual aids we know. First of all, if your charts are prepared in advance and fastened together in a pad, you run no risk of showing any of them out of the proper order—a big plus.

But there are many other advantages. Listed below are a few of the more important ones.

- Flipcharts are not subject to the whims of mechanical or electrical failure. (Of course, we *have* seen them fall off the stand. And we have even seen the stand collapse!)

- Flipcharts can be used almost anywhere, so long as the audience is not too large. Remember that the words must be large enough and spaced so they are readable from the back of the room.

- Flipcharts can be prepared simply and inexpensively. (On the other hand, they *can* be quite expensive, should you decide to go first class by employing a professional artist.)

- Flipcharts can be readily turned back to reemphasize important points or to summarize an entire presentation quickly.

- Flipcharts can give your memory an *extra* boost. Not only will the information on the chart itself help you stay on track, but, if you like, you can pencil in any additional facts you need, right on the chart. Do it very lightly, so you can read at close range, but the audience won't be able to see from the greater distance. This system is fully as effective as cue cards.

- Flipcharts are used with houselights "up." This means that you, the speaker, are in full command. You are always in plain sight of the audience, so that you don't play "second fiddle" to your visuals. Also, you can *see* the audience and get instant feedback by observing their reactions and how well they are paying attention. That's an important consideration — they can even go to sleep without your knowing it when the lights are out for a slide presentation!

- Flipcharts, although bulky, are light and easy to transport. More important, they are *unbreakable*. (The charts themselves, that is. The stand is another matter.)

Okay, are there *minuses?*

Yes, there are a few. First of all, unless your artwork is truly outstanding, the effect of the flipcharts on the audience usually falls short of "smashing." Because the charts are simple and easy, they unfortunately *appear to be* simple and easy to the audience. They can do the job fine, but the usual garden varieties don't have much pizzazz.

And, as we hinted earlier, they don't work adequately except before small, intimate audiences. If you use flipcharts in a large hall or auditorium, the participants in the back row will probably never find out what you were talking about.

Next, having told you that flipcharts are easy to transport, we must now revise the statement and say that it isn't universally true. They are easy to carry *if you have a car.* They are awkward and bulky for public transportation or for carrying aboard an aircraft. (And on this latter point, if you've had any brushes with Murphy's Law, you know that you had better keep your presentation materials with you and carry them on the plane. Check them through, and inevitably you will get to the show, but your graphics won't. Or — God forbid, vice versa.)

Chalkboards

In the "olden days," we used to call these things "blackboards." Now the term is no longer accurate, since they are likely to be just about any color, or even white. (Indeed, the white ones are among the best, if you get the kind that permit you to use brightly colored, washable crayons or felt-tip markers.)

In this age of technology and high prices, many presenters have been led to think that the only way to demonstrate anything effectively is to use complex equipment.

Folks, it just ain't so. Teachers have been doing a thoroughly effective job with the good old-fashioned chalkboard for a long, long time.

The chalkboard has many built-in advantages. For example:

- You can be confident that it's ready *all* the time. Like the flipchart, it has no fuses to blow or bulbs to burn out. (But don't forget to wash it once in a while.)

- You don't have to be a skilled artist to use it. And if you make a mistake, it is easy to erase.
- You don't have to worry about timing or synchronizing, as you do with slides. You can pace yourself as quickly or as slowly as you want to.
- You can achieve the effect of spontaneity, even if you have planned every word in advance.
- You can use the chalkboard as a device for gaining audience involvement. Ask the audience for comments or suggestions; then write them on the board for discussion.
- You can show progressive developments with great effectiveness. Achieve a cumulative "build-up" simply by writing down each idea or process as your oral description goes on.

But, there are a few disadvantages.

- Chalkboards are inadequate for showing fine detail. They work best when you employ some degree of simplification.
- Chalkboards may not be sufficiently visible to be properly seen by a large audience.
- Chalkboards can be totally ineffective if the demonstrator's handwriting is not sufficiently large, firm, clear, and legible.

Magnetic Chalkboards. In recent years, even the old-fashioned chalkboard has been updated. Nowadays they are manufactured out of various materials that at first blush seem inappropriate or unlikely—for example, one very popular type these days is made out of a sheet of stainless steel, coated with a porcelainlike finish. This combination serves a dual purpose: you can not only mark on the porcelain surface, but you can also use it as you would a bulletin board—or even display three-dimensional materials—by using magnets. This handy arrangement does away with messy taping or thumbtacks.

Also, you can combine techniques, writing or drawing on the display surface with your magic markers, and sticking on bulletin-board types of materials with magnets.

Study the manufacturers' and retailers' catalogs for accessories to be used with magnetic chalkboards. You may be surprised to find how many different types of magnetic holders are available: frames, pointers, arrows, and a wide assortment of other shapes and configurations, with an equally wide choice of sizes and colors.

The Big "No-No" of Chalkboards. Public school teachers have known, probably since the dawn of education, that it is not a good idea to turn one's back on a class.

Okay, you probably won't have to worry about spitballs when you are putting on your presentation, but the psychology of facing your audience is still important.

We accordingly suggest that when you write on the chalkboard, always stand "crabwise" (for want of a better term), at least partially facing your viewers. Keep your body to the side of their line of vision—that way, everyone can see what you are writing while you are doing it.

Quite frankly, this advice, while sound, is a "do what we say, not what we do." We don't always observe this rule ourselves. Maybe it is simply the arrogance that can stem from long practice and overfamiliarity. We excuse ourselves by saying that we are in good company—we know some first-rate presenters who habitually break this rule; they blithely write away with their backs aimed directly at the audience—and it appears that they carry it off quite well. So, if you're supremely self-confident, go ahead and turn your back. But don't say we didn't warn you.

Flannelboards

Flannelboards enjoyed a brief moment of glory a few years back, and they remain one of the options open to you. In effect, they are similar to magnetic chalkboards, and are suitable for displaying the same general types of material. Only the principle is different—the display surface is a board covered with flannel, to which the displayed items easily adhere.

Mock-ups and Models

Now it's time to explain, as we promised at the beginning of the chapter, why we changed the order of presentation, skipping over the discussion of mock-ups and models until now.

We changed the order deliberately because mock-ups, particularly, are considered "oddballs" in most presentations. (This is not to say that they cannot be valuable teaching aids, in the right circumstances.) We've used them occasionally (although not all that often) to advantage, but many presenters might go through life without ever using either a mock-up or a model.

What, incidentally, is the difference?

Primarily, a mock-up is not intended to be an exact copy of an original. It may contain only the particular parts to be studied or discussed; these may be enlarged in detail, or in many cases, highly simplified. A mock-up may or may not have moving parts.

A model is supposed to show every part, every detail of the original, with the prime difference being that of size. The model is usually scaled down (or up) by a specific ratio.

At the Apollo prelaunch briefings held at Cape Kennedy (put on for the VIP guests before each of the moon launches) an important part of the presentation was a life-size model (not a mock-up) of the Lunar Module. The astronaut who served as the master of ceremonies (not, of course, one of those scheduled for the mission) would at one point in the program demonstrate to the audience an enactment of the descent to the moon's surface.

Many persons commented that the demonstration was extremely interesting and effective. But some questioned the economics—obviously such a model had to be very expensive. The fact is, NASA had the model anyway; it had been built for training purposes. The agency would not have built a life-size model just for a presentation, no matter how prestigious or important.

The moral of this, if there is one, is simple: If you happen to have a suitable model or mock-up readily available, by all means take advantage of it. They *are* effective when properly used.

But if you don't have them on hand, chances are you won't miss them.

When to Use Electronic Media

Things seen are mightier than things heard.
— ALFRED, LORD TENNYSON

Advantages of Projection Equipment

For many meeting planners, the mention of a presentation automatically brings to mind the use of projection techniques. They know from experience that for maximum benefit of graphics before large audiences, projection is just about the only way to go. We agree that projection is hard to beat — so long as you avoid the pitfalls, of which there are plenty.

Projection gives a greater choice and range of visual material than does any other visual aid. But the number one benefit is that projection devices permit you to blow up your graphics to a large enough size to be seen by hundreds of viewers at the same time. That's a mighty big plus.

Furthermore, they offer you a wide variety of options — you can illustrate ideas by drawing pictures, using handwriting, printing, cartoons, photographs, or whatever. The only thing holding you back is a lack of imagination on your part.

On top of all this, it is usually a simple matter to add sound, whether it be music, special effects, or a simple narration either in your own voice or that of a professional speaker.

Using color. Projection systems also offer many easy and effective ways of employing color. However, the user must handle color contrasts with special care, especially in slide art. (See Chapter 22 for a more extensive discussion of color in slide art.)

Many of the books on slide presentations are pretty tough about the restrictions. Some go so far as to recommend limiting the number of colors; essentially, they demand that users not deviate in the slightest from that recommended list. We think this approach is faintly ridiculous: Far better to experiment and check things out for yourself. Find out to your own satisfaction what will work and what won't.

Both of us have had special, fancy transparencies — prepared by excellent artists — that didn't show up as well as might have been expected. The problem was usually that the lettering did not present sufficient contrast against the background. Unless all overhead lights are turned out, this kind of lettering washes out and won't show up clearly enough to be read.

The best way to find out what will work, we repeat, is to try. You can ruin the psyches of your entire art department if you hang too many restrictions on their choices of color. You need their good will, so for goodness sake don't go out of your way to make them bitter. Remember that subtle use of color is part of the artist's stock in trade.

Rear-screen projection. A frequently cited criticism of projection (we'll discuss it more later) is the need for a darkened room. Well, this is another criticism that "ain't necessarily so." Many well-equipped conference rooms these days are fitted with special diffusion-type screens that make it possible to project slides and motion pictures from the rear. A respectably bright image can be projected right through the screen without completely darkening the room.

Frankly, we like rear projection systems very much. They do away with the room light problem, and also with most of the distraction of a whirring projector, or of having the beam of light interfered with by the shadows of latecomers trying to sneak in.

Rear projection is seen most often, however, in miniaturized "table-top" form. Salespeople and other presenters can easily carry everything they need to make a presentation, all neatly packaged in a small suitcase or an attaché case.

Table-top systems are also popular for automatically repeated presentations at trade shows and the like. But don't let your imagination be limited by this side discussion—rear projection can be extremely successful even in large auditoriums, assuming that the installation has been properly designed.

Drawbacks of Projection

As we've said earlier, a projector can "steal your show" if you don't watch out. Once the overhead lights are turned off, you're no longer the center-stage attraction—your visuals are. You risk becoming just a disembodied voice.

That's not the only problem. If the screen is behind you and you are trying to narrate and synchronize with the material appearing on the screen, you'll have a Hobson's Choice. Either turn away from the audience (we've already explained that's a bad technique) so you can get your cues, or keep facing the audience and risk missing those cues. To add to the difficulty, if you're close to the screen and the pictures are large, you can't see what's going on very well. The only answer is *rehearsal*—lots of it. With enough practice, you'll get the timing right.

We'd be less than realistic if we didn't warn you about one more potential problem. We both spent time in the military service and had to watch interminable (and incredibly dull) training films. We, like most of our fellows, found that the fine dark auditorium was a great place to catch up on a little shuteye. The droning narrations, the hum of the projector, can be as soporific as a glass of warm milk. It's fun to look around the auditorium the second after the houselights come up and see how many heads nearly snap off!

Using Overhead Projectors

Speaking of the military, that's where we first saw the use of overhead projectors. During World War II, these innovative devices were considered very advanced (rightly so), and servicemen were confronted with them everywhere then and for years to come.

They are no longer a novelty, but they still work fine, with many advantages. Some of these are:

- You don't need an operator to run the machine. The simplest and best approach is usually to do it yourself.

- You can keep the overhead lights on and face the audience; most (but not all) overhead projectors are powerful enough to show clear images in full room light.

- You can point out features appearing on the screen by pointing at the materials as they lie on the light table of the projector; this method is easier and less obtrusive than trying to use a pointer at the projected image on the screen.

- You can draw or write on clear plastic lying on the light table (the clear plastic—not you!) so that you are *creating* a visual right before the eyes of the audience. Using colored markers, you can produce some dramatic effects with surprisingly simple methods.

- You are in total control of the pace of the show and can handle *all* effects directly, without having to ask anyone for assistance.

- You can draw upon a variety of special effects, including a very useful one called the "overlay." This involves preparing a series of drawings, with succeeding stages drawn on separate clear (or colored) plastic sheets. Thus developments or changes can be depicted one step at a time. We will tell you how to do this, and how to make excellent transparencies (sometimes called "overhead cells") quickly, easily, and inexpensively, in later chapters.

Disadvantages of overhead projectors. The first disadvantage of overhead projectors that we'll mention here is common to any kind of projection visuals. Namely, the users are sorely tempted to rely too heavily on the visuals. They just project them up there on the screen and read them word for word to the audience. At best this is boring. At worst, it's a disaster. Here are a few more things to watch out for:

- Although it's easy to make good transparencies, it's easier to make bad ones—even terrible ones. You have seen plenty of these visual disasters, and so have we. Somebody takes a faded fifth carbon copy of a letter, for example, and makes a miserable, washed-out, overcrowded transparency that nobody can read.

- Speakers often yield to the temptation of leaving the projector going all the time. This is a distraction—not an aid.

- Some projectors (including some of the ultralight and compact briefcase models that shine the light down from the top) simply will not project a bright enough image to show up in an undarkened room. If you have such a machine, you might as well recognize the necessity of turning out the lights. Remember, if the audience can't see and read your visuals clearly and easily, the whole effect is negative—far worse than not using visuals at all.

- Orientation of the projector to the screen is critical. Because of the short focal length, you have to make sure the projector is exactly at right angles to the screen. You must be almost equally careful of the vertical angle. Otherwise, there will be severe distortion, called "keystoning."

- You may have to furnish your own projector. Almost every organization before which you might appear will have a 35mm projector. But overhead projectors, although fairly popular, are not so likely to "come with the room." And bringing your own projector isn't all that much fun, either. The good ones are often somewhat bulky and heavy, and the light portables project an inferior image.

- You need to practice getting the overheads on and off smoothly, without irritating the audience with frequent flashes of "raw light" on the screen. We suggest labeling the transparencies along the edge to show correct orientation. (Jeff has been using transparencies for years, but being a slow learner, still tends to put them on upside down.)

That looks like an extensive list of drawbacks, but please don't be discouraged. As it happens, we both like overhead transparencies very much. We consider them to be among the most effective choices you can make, and urge that you consider the pros and cons carefully. There's an excellent chance you may wind up using overheads for your next presentation.

Using Slide Projectors

All this talk and here we are just now getting around to slides—the medium that many meeting planners consider "the only way to go." They have good reason; slide presentations offer many benefits.

Advantages of slides. We don't really have enough space to tell you *all* the advantages of slides, but these are typical:

- You can present them to audiences of any size; if regular 35mm slides won't cut it, you can go to "superslides." As a last resort, you can try using the old-fashioned 2 x 2 glass "lantern slides."

- You can use a very wide range of subject matter, techniques, and art treatments.

- You can use full color very easily, and with relatively little additional expense. Color photography of excellent quality is relatively inexpensive when compared to other forms of art preparation.

- You can carry an entire slide show in a relatively small package or case.

- You can make all the duplicates you want from each slide original, again, at relatively low cost.

- You can change slides around easily if you want to rearrange or rejigger your presentation. It's easy to add or delete at a moment's notice.

- You can fit your presentation—slides and talk—to your individual audiences, the room environment, and so on.

- You can almost always borrow or rent a suitable projector without having to carry your own.

Sounds pretty good, right?

By this time, though, you surely won't be surprised when we take time out to tell you a few of the drawbacks.

Drawbacks of slides

- You have to watch out constantly for mixed-up slides, or slides that have been inserted backwards or upside down. We'll tell you how to avoid this in Chapter 15, but it often happens to most of us anyway.

- You can have a slide projector that works perfectly during the trial runs, but will refuse to advance the slides, or will stick, or go out of focus, when you finally do the real show (Murphy's Law).

- You have to turn out the lights (unless you use a rear projector). This means you lose a certain amount of your rapport with, and control of, the group.

- You may have to use an assistant to control the mechanics of the slide presentation. This means there can easily be some missed cues—or worse.

- You can't rush in last-minute changes to artwork the way you can with overhead transparencies. Making, copying, and duplicating slides takes more time.

Using Filmstrip Projectors

If you have a slide presentation that has been thoroughly shaken down, and you feel that it can be used in future showings in the same order and format, you may want to consider putting the show in filmstrip form—particularly if you need a number of copies and the projection equipment is available.

Essentially, filmstrips are slide shows in which the slides have been transferred onto a continuous roll or strip of 35mm film much like motion picture film. Handle them with the same care you would use for the latter—to avoid scratching and finger marking, touch only the edges and stay away from the picture surfaces.

Filmstrip projectors are available in a variety of styles and models, such as "autoload" and "cartridge" types, self-contained sound filmstrip projectors, and rear-screen projectors for individual viewing. Obviously, while many of these types would be useful for training, they are not appropriate for meeting presentations.

(One good use for sound filmstrips is for static, or standing, lobby displays. The sound track, usually on tape, sends an inaudible "beeper" signal to the projector to advance each frame. With a continuous film loop, such a projector can function unattended.)

With a few notable exceptions, filmstrips share the advantages and disadvantages of regular slides. An extra advantage of filmstrips is that your show won't get out of sequence, and once the strip is properly loaded, there is no danger of showing frames backwards or upside down. On the negative side, you can't change the order of any of the pictures or add new ones, as you can with separate slides. Also, it is difficult (if not impossible) to back up. Reverse movement of the filmstrip for more than a frame or two is likely to jam the machine.

Using Motion Picture Projectors

Motion pictures offer a seemingly easy way of sparking a presentation and cutting down the time that the presenter must be "on stage." And a motion picture, when well done, is a marvelously effective device. If you have a first-rate film available that fits your purpose, by all means use it. (We don't propose to tell you how to make your own do-It-yourself movie here. That subject calls for an entire book, not just a few paragraphs of discussion.)

Let us emphasize, especially, that you should exercise great care in choosing motion picture films. Powerful as the medium is when the film is well done, it is just as powerful at ruining your meeting if the film is unsuitable for the occasion. If your experience is anything like ours, you've seen far too many films—usually training films—that are good for nothing but putting the viewers to sleep.

Why would anyone show such films in the first place? We suspect that in many cases a sin of omission is involved: the presenter has simply ordered the film from a catalog description and shown it without taking the trouble to preview it. This is perhaps the greatest single mistake you can make. *Always* preview any film you plan to show publicly, and look at it with a stern and critical eye to ensure that it is up to the required standard to do the job. This is also the time to learn any bad news—for instance, that the reel of film may have bad splices or "jumps" in the sound track caused by sloppy film repairing. *Don't leave this important previewing task to anyone else!*

Hazards of using movies. Insofar as the use of motion pictures is concerned, the problems are somewhat similar to those encountered with slide and filmstrip shows, but with a couple of additional hazards. The first is mechanical: improperly threaded film can be damaged (scratched, sprockets torn, etc.) beyond repair before the operator even becomes aware something has gone wrong. Be sure you (or your operator—chances are you won't be running the projector yourself) work with the equipment in advance and become thoroughly familiar with the way it operates.

Make sure the film is loaded with great care, even when using a so-called automatic loader. We've seen sprockets ripped to shreds when the film leader was not properly seated at the beginning of the loading process.

Another hazard is that the film may break during the showing, especially if it has been spliced. When I (Jeff) was doing the Apollo VIP briefings at Cape Kennedy, we had several horrendous experiences with motion picture projectors. On one occasion, we had multiple showings going on at various locations, and this required using not only all our regular prints, but even the "master" copy from which the other prints had been made. The master film was, of course, full of splices, as it had been made up from a number of 16mm sequences NASA had shot during astronaut training. We ran the film through before the briefing to make sure it was okay, and it ran fine. I'm still not sure what happened, but when we had the actual briefing, there was one embarrassing moment after another. If the film managed to get past one splice without breaking, I don't know when it was!

The moral is: *Don't use masters for projection—ever!* (Not only is there the risk of splices coming loose—but the cost is too high if you damage the master.)

Another hazard we encountered with these multiple showings was that we had to send out some operators and presenters who were not familiar with the show. (We furnished them all the film and other A/V materials and a copy of the script, and told them to rehearse, but some of them didn't.) And I heard of one case in which they didn't have a large enough take-up reel on the projector, and had to spool off hundreds of feet of film onto the floor.

A final caution: If the film does break during the showing, don't try to make a temporary splice or other repair on the spot. Instead, overlap the broken film onto the take-up reel on top of the other film already on the reel. Mark the place where the film has broken with a slip of paper, and continue running the film.

After the showing is over, *do not rewind the film.* Leave it on the take-up reel, and return it to technicians who have the skill and equipment to repair it properly.

Some film tips from Chuck Waterman. My associate, Chuck Waterman, is experienced in all phases of film, including scriptwriting and production. Here are some tips from him that he suggested I put in at this point:

Chuck says that, unless you want to impress your audience with your positively amateur standing as a presenter, you will *always:*

- Set up and run your film before the audience arrives, "boresighting" it precisely on the screen. Nothing gives you a low rating with the audience quicker than having to fool around with the projector after you've started it running.

- Rewind the film back to the starting point (usually just before the title). A good way to do this is, after rewinding, to show the countdown clock on the screen and kill the projector right after the last audible beep. When you turn the projector on again, the film will start smoothly into the title, using the fade-in that is normally provided for the purpose. This avoids socking your audience with a bright title scene in a darkened room, and it provides the proper segue of sound that was built into the title background.

- Check the sound level. During your rehearsal, let the machine run with the sound on; then walk around the room and check audibility. Play it slightly louder than you need it, because with an audience present, some of the sound energy will be absorbed by the bodies. *Never* fiddle with the sound knob during show projection!

- During the showing of the film, make sure the operator stays with the equipment. Even good machines running film in good condition will sometimes develop the jitters, causing a horrid twitching of the visual image. Usually, gentle finger pressure on the film pressure plate will correct the condition and allow the show to continue without stopping the machine. If the trouble is serious, stop the show: the projector may be chewing gigantic gaps in the film where the sprocket holes are supposed to be.

- Remember that the *image* is projected through the lens, called the picture head, and the *sound* is taken off at the sound head, twenty-six frames ahead of the image on 16mm films (twenty frames on 35mm films). Trouble can develop in two ways because of this:

  —A poorly spliced film from which more than one or two frames have been removed will be "out of sync" in sight and sound. The sound picked off by the sound head will be for the image somewhere later than the twenty-six (or twenty) frames then being shown. This results in poor "lip sync" and causes audiences to be annoyed by the difference in visual and aural effects.
  —A film that is mounted improperly on the projector may have too tight or too loose a loop between sound and picture heads. Just as with badly spliced film, the prescribed image-sound interval is lost and lip sync is ruined.

- Have the operator keep an eye peeled for a slipping take-up reel drive chain. If this goes unnoticed, yards of film may wind up on the floor or, worse, wrapped around the axle of the take-up reel. Occasionally, the feed reel will lurch ahead and cause a loop to form before the film enters the feed sprocket that pulls the film through the projector. If the lurching is only minor and infrequent, you may be able to live with the problem. But if the feed reel sticks on each revolution, or the film seems to have a hard time getting out of the reel, you may be working with a bent reel. This is hard on the film and may create serious difficulties during projection.

- If the projector you are using permits you to run the speaker up behind or beside the screen, do so. The closer image and sound come from the same location, the better. Audiences are accustomed to hearing projectors running behind or beside them, but quality shows should be projected with image and sound doing everything they can for you, *together.*

- As with any equipment requiring power and speaker cables, tape the lines firmly to the floor or wall so people won't trip over them or kick them in the dark. Anchoring cords by making two turns around the table leg near the projector helps prevent a sudden disconnect by someone's stepping on the cord.

- Make sure your operator has an extra projection bulb and exciter (sound head) lamp. Changing either of these during a show calls for a cool head and technical know-how. A good operator keeps a flashlight handy and knows exactly the sequence of actions to follow when a quick bulb or lamp change is necessary. (The first step is to unplug the power!)

- If disaster strikes (bad bulb or lamp, film "bloating" caused by a stuck frame in the projection gate, or—heaven forbid!—a fire in the film gate because the film can't get through), try to keep your show going while the technician fixes the problem. Some brief comment such as, "I'm fortunate to have George (or Mary) operating the equipment tonight. Until he (or she) gets it operating again, let me . . ." and here you make a comment about the film that's been seen so far or ask a question. *Get the audience's attention away from the operator.* Keep your act going until you get the signal that everything is ready to resume projection. *Don't* engage in a dialogue. You should have silent signals that you and your operator have practiced, so that your showmanship does not end up being a show of your panic!

Using Videotape

Videotape is becoming increasingly popular, and deservedly so. Until recent years, the cost of color cameras was so outrageously high that most of us who have to operate on low budgets restricted ourselves to black-and-white. This is no longer necessary.

A well-produced videotape can be used in many cases the same way that a motion picture film would be. In this case, do-it-yourself productions are much easier and far less expensive. If you make a mistake, you haven't lost a huge investment; you just erase the tape and shoot again.

For training purposes, videotape is often ideal. My partner, Lou Hampton, is a professional speech coach. When he videotapes one of his clients and plays the tape back for critique, he gets very little argument!

The low-priced "home-style" video recorders (either Beta format or VHS) use a cassette in which the tape is ½-inch wide. The quality, while excellent, is not up to professional production standards. If you plan to use videotape for a major presentation, stick to the ¾-inch U-Matic format; or, if your budget and facilities permit, 1-inch broadcast-quality tape.

Again, we don't have the space here to go into production detail. Do some reading on the subject. But better still, shoot lots of tape. The erasable feature means that it costs you very little to practice, and there is nothing like experience.

Using Videodiscs

We have mixed feelings about videodiscs. At the time of this writing, there are several competing systems, each with certain advantages and disadvantages. (Sort of like the long-ago conflict between 33⅓ records and 45s. Eventually, each found its place in the market.) A shake-down process is now going on, and perhaps will be resolved soon, but we're not counting on it.

The advantages of videodisc are several: first, the clarity of the pictures is extraordinary—far superior to that of tape; second, the sound is on a stereo track, which means that not only is the sound superior to that of tape, but the system permits refinements such as having a foreign language translation on the second track; third, by means of computer techniques, a particular frame on the disc can be located almost instantly and projected as a still picture. Theoretically, it's possible to put the contents of all the major art galleries of the world on one or two videodiscs. The possibilities are exciting.

But this medium is not in broad distribution as we write this. Available programs are limited, and, of course, you cannot make your own, as you can with a tape. For specific purposes, the disc approach is fine, but we are inclined to stick with tape until the discs have time to mature a bit.

Preparing the Agenda

If you don't know where you are going,
you'll probably end up somewhere else.

—LAURENCE J. PETER

The "Chinese Method"

Many mystery writers plot a good ending, then work backwards and plan the rest of the book. This system, sometimes called the "Chinese Method," deserves your attention. It works extremely well when you are planning the agenda for your meeting. Here's how:

Pretend the meeting is over and the guests are leaving. What message should they be carrying away with them, and how would you like them to feel about that message?

But to start at the ending, you still have to do one other thing first—and that's to analyze the audience.

Audience—Finding the Common Denominator

What kind of persons will make up your audience? Bosses? Customers? Sales force? Students? Trainers? Teachers? Mixed group?

Whatever the make-up of the group, it's your job to find the common denominator. And to do that, you must know *exactly* what you want to accomplish.

Remember this—in your mind's eye, the audience and your purpose must be as one.

In 1969, one of the greatest audiences ever assembled attended the VIP briefing presented at Cape Kennedy the night before Apollo 11 lifted off for the first moon landing mission. As you might imagine, almost everybody who was anybody here and abroad attended, from the very top leaders of the United States and most of the free (and not-so-free) world, right on down through American and foreign diplomats, legislators, celebrities of television, stage, and screen, and heaven knows who else.

What was the purpose of the briefing? What was the important message for them to take home with them? Primarily, to give an understanding of the moon exploration mission and the many benefits that would result from it. But there were also some other, less obvious, purposes. In a manner of speaking, NASA had something to sell—the space program itself. The subject is one that is much misunderstood, and NASA briefers felt this was an excellent opportunity to enlighten the participants. There was nothing surreptitious; the motivation was of the highest—as high as mankind's noblest aspirations.

In simple terms, the product NASA was trying to sell was progress. That's an extremely valuable product, but it's not easily salable if the potential customers can't be made to understand its worth.

Customers don't always know what they want, and that's bad enough. But far worse, they quite often don't even know what they *need,* or to put it in the terms of benevolent "big brother"—what's good for them!

The NASA briefing intended to show the audience why the space program is so important. It was designed to explain what space research is doing for people everywhere—its manifold values in dollars and cents—in human lives saved—in new knowledge acquired—in new methods and materials developed—in new benefits for ourselves and for all of humanity.

Was it a con job? Was NASA trying to fool or defraud the American public? Was the agency trying to sell a worthless bill of goods?

No way. Don't think of that monstrous idea for one moment.

The NASA team felt then—and still feels today—that they were offering the most useful and valuable product in all history.

How did they merchandise the idea? And did they succeed? Probably not—at least the evidence shows that the space budget was cut back sharply not long after the moon landings were completed.

Nevertheless, that night NASA had a chance to zero in on a specific audience, and those NASA officials present truly believed they had convinced that audience. Those who *understood* the message *believed* the message. And therein lies the key.

Prepare Your Audience

Maybe that last sentence overstates the case a trifle. Probably we should have said "part of the key." The rest—and just as important—is to *prepare* your audience so that it will be ready for, and receptive to, your message.

In a way, we might consider the situation as being analogous to that of an advertising campaign.

The purpose of a presentation is to sell an attitude or an idea to the participants. *But*—the purpose of the preliminary work is to sell the audience on the notion that they want to know more about the "product" you are going to sell them. Outlined below are a series of steps that will help you accomplish your aims.

Step one—"teasers." Send out "teasers" (designed to stir up interest) well before the event is to take place. Many meeting planners use mottoes or logos for their meetings, and to fit the theme they send some cheap but useful gifts as teasers. For example, a pen and pencil set inscribed "Writing with Precision," or a set of golf tees mounted on a card with the meeting logo "Tee off on tomorrow," or whatever.

Give plenty of advance notice on what the meeting is about, when and where it will be held, how long it will last, recommended methods of transportation, and premeeting assignments or preparations.

Step two—premeeting assignments. Participants can more easily apply what they learn if you prepare premeeting assignments so they can work to achieve specific objectives.

And here goes your "sales pitch" again:

Stress what the benefits are going to be: improved status, more pleasure from the job, a sense of accomplishment, increased productivity, or making the job easier. (Maybe you can add others of your own.)

Assignments given well before a meeting actually begins will increase the interest of the participants. You get a double-barreled benefit, for the assignments serve also as an important and useful form of training.

In the seminars on "Writing with Precision," the seminar leader has the participants write (in advance) a short autobiography to hand in before the first meeting. This tells the instructor a lot about the participants, making them mean much more than just a roomful of name tags and job titles. At the same time, the instructor gets a good preview of the participants' individual writing styles and any serious problems they may have in getting their words down on paper.

There are, of course, many kinds of assignments that can be given out in advance. Here are a few examples.

- Lists of required or recommended reading
- Material to be prepared for presentation at the meeting
- Questionnaires asking specifics about the needs and expectations of the participants

Doubtless you can think of others.

Step three—preliminary handouts. Some experts doubt the wisdom of giving participants any handouts or reading material in advance of the meeting. Their logic goes something like this:

1. You may take away from the surprise element or the mystery of the show itself by giving away some of the ingredients ahead of time.
2. You may divide the attention of your audience. They may end up reading handouts at a time when you want them to be listening to you.

Both these objections can be valid. We say "can be" because there are ways you can beat them. Here's how:

For objection No. 1, you simply use handouts in advance that will not "telegraph your punches." Put in items that are useful or important, but not your real haymakers. Save those for appropriate, well-timed high spots in the meeting proper.

For objection No. 2, simply don't *overdo* the advance handouts. Keep the quantity down to a reasonable limit. Reserve other handouts to be given out singly, *when you need them,* and *after* you have completed the oral presentation introducing the material covered.

Step four—plan postmeeting assignments. Be sure that in your overall plan you look past the meeting itself. You must use every opportunity to see that the information gained by participants will be put to the best possible use. If new techniques were introduced in the meeting, for example, you should have a follow-up plan to give assignments that will help participants put these techniques into operation. Remember: the more carefully and thoroughly you plan, and the more specifically you lay out the assignments, the better the results you are going to achieve.

Tailoring the Script to the Audience

You need a "grabber" to get the attention of your audience. But don't waste your biggest, best blockbuster of an idea on the opening pitch.

You may be tempted, but resist the temptation. At that point in the proceeding you would almost undoubtedly be wasting some of your best ammunition.

In the book *Writing with Precision,* Jeff stresses getting straight to the point, advising readers to put their most important items and ideas right up front. In *written* communications, this approach works great; we recommend it heartily.

But meetings and oral presentations are a different ballgame. In the first place, audience attention is always very high at the beginning. It will stay high for a time, automatically, unless the speaker does something so downright awful or dull that it turns off the audience. Be aware, however, that such things *have* happened, and can happen again.

So—start out on a high note (but not the highest) and concentrate on getting and holding your audience's attention. Set their minds at ease by telling them why they are present and explaining (briefly) what they can expect.

But—don't fall into the trap of beginning your talk with the most important topic, then moving on in descending order of importance. Inevitably, you'll spend too much time on the early topics and find yourself "painted into a corner" with no alternative but to end the meeting on a weak note. Always remember: *bring out your strongest points just before the coffee and meal breaks and at the close of the meeting.* This gives participants time to gnaw on the big stuff a while before you introduce a new topic.

Take a tip from show business and you'll automatically do a better job of spacing your topics. In a three-act musical stage production, the "big song" is hinted at in the beginning, featured at the end of the second act right before intermission, and then highlighted in the finale.

So—intersperse the important points at intervals throughout the meeting. Since the last things said are those that are remembered best, be sure to end with a strong finale.

Change from topic to topic with smooth, logical transitions. Insert highlights throughout; as you develop each topic, seek ways to include visual aids, demonstrations, and audience involvement. Decide what props will be necessary for the meeting and prepare them for use. Always keep in mind a cardinal rule of group speaking:

> *If they can't hear it—don't say it!*
> *If they can't see it—don't show it!*

Preparing Yourself as a Speaker

The best visual on the podium is you.

　　　　　　　　　— BUD REBEDEAU

The Importance of Rehearsing

Leading a meeting effectively requires a combination of skills; when you put them all together smoothly (as Chuck Waterman says, "so the seams don't show"), you'll almost automatically reach your objectives with and through the group.

There is only one sure way to do this: *rehearse!* Prepare yourself adequately, and become so thoroughly familiar with your material that you can project it with composure and confidence.

How you rehearse is important. Don't think, as many do, that you just need to go over the words. To bring your presentation to life, whenever possible you should duplicate the conditions of your planned performance: that means in the actual room, on the podium, using the props and demonstrations, all the voice inflections, and all the actions, *just as you expect to perform in front of the group.*

Before you get your presentation up to the point of trying it in the actual room, you may wish to rehearse in your office or at home in front of one or more persons. But when you think you have it down pat, get a competent evaluator to go with you, and take your rehearsal into the actual meeting room so you can practice in the environment, get used to the sound of your own voice in it, and familiarize yourself with all the physical patterns involved in your presentation, such as walking to the chalkboard or chart tablet.

Keep in mind that in every meeting you have a hidden agenda as well as a printed agenda. Your hidden agenda is to project an image of confidence, authority, and credibility. What you say and how you say it are equally important.

To help you get the most out of your hidden agenda, we will share some thoughts with you on scripts, stage presence, and voice effectiveness.

These are not singular thoughts. Many of the ideas presented in the next few pages came through consultation with Bud Rebedeau and from material that Bud uses in his workshop, "Meeting Dynamics."

Scripts, Outlines, Notes

Few executive speakers deliver the same speech often enough to make an effective presentation without some written guide. The discipline of a written structure discourages rambling. Following a well-prepared written script, outline, or notes allows a sharp, logical presentation that makes and supports major points and reaches objectives quickly. Of course, if your supporting visuals are controlled by a second party, you must use a word-for-word delivery.

Whether you speak from a script, an outline, or from 3 x 5 inch notecards, one basic standard applies—they must be readable! Scribbled remarks are difficult, if not impossible, to read as you talk. Trying to make sense from quickly scribbled notes can disrupt the timing of your presentation. During script preparation, it's all too easy to fall into the trap of just scribbling. Avoid it!

Here are some typing tips that will give you the readability you need:

- Leave a 2½-inch left margin.
- Use an "orator" or "speech" typeface—extra-large print for easy reading.
- Double-space between lines—four spaces between paragraphs.
- End pages at the end of paragraphs—no split paragraphs from one page to another.
- Number the pages bottom center.
- Allow at least four blank lines on top of the first page to add current notes or "pickups" from previous speakers.

With typed pages in hand, you are ready to complete your preparation. Here are some techniques professionals use:

1. Deliver the script aloud and make necessary word changes. Some words "read" well but don't "talk" easily. The same holds true for sentences. Avoid those containing too many of the same consonants close together. Here's an example I came across recently:

    > The cherry blossoms rustled; a brace of dogs barked like brass being beaten; a brown and white butterfly darted erratically along the top of the grass, a blithe dancer without a partner.*

    As *written* prose, that reads beautifully. Now *say* it. Even if your tongue doesn't trip you up with the series of "b" words in a row, the passage just simply loses something in the translation to the spoken sounds: this makes an excellent demonstration of how reading aloud helps you identify and alter such passages.

2. Read with a pencil. Insert "pacing" marks (one slash for comma, two slashes for period). Underline "hit" words to be stressed. Print marginal notes to yourself (slowly—pause here—distribute prop here, and so on).

3. Shorten "too-long" sentences.

4. Eliminate jargon unfamiliar to the audience.

Your overt objective is to reach a clear goal through the members of the group. Your covert objective is to project a leadership image of confidence, authority, clarity, and warmth. *How* you present it is equally as important to your image as *what* you present.

*Eric Van Lustbader, *The Ninja*, Fawcett Crest, New York, 1980, p. 160.

Stage Presence

How you look, act, talk, and control the attention of the group contributes powerfully to the overall impact you make. If you appear calm, composed, and confident, your message will get through to the group as having warmth, authority, and sincerity. If you appear timid or ill at ease, your message will sound weak—lacking importance and credibility.

Your task as presenter is to achieve the calm, confident look that bespeaks authority. Your clothes and your language make an important statement about yourself. Because of our human need for what Bud calls "predictive accuracy," we are most comfortable with people most like ourselves. Clothes and language that are not appropriate for the group and the situation create an unnecessary obstacle for the presenter. On the other hand, appropriate dress and appropriate language foster confidence.

As well as looking the part, you must act the part. Confidence and *controlled* enthusiasm are the key. Appropriate body language will reinforce your words. In fact, these visual clues often tell the audience more clearly how you feel about the message than do your words. Repetitive, nervous mannerisms are distracting and betray lack of confidence. When the group sees constant adjusting of eyeglasses, jingling change in pockets, ear pulling, or nose scratching, it will try to decide whether you lack confidence in yourself or in your material.

A speaker who talks in a near monotone and has a locked-in, "frozen" stance tells the audience something else: a lack of enthusiasm, an attitude of take it or leave it. The audience must decide whether the cause is your stage fright or your lack of interest in your proposal.

A group is nearly always sympathetic to you, the speaker. It wants you to be a good presenter. If you are well-prepared, deliver well-organized material with confidence, and have an appropriate amount of enthusiasm, you can expect to win confidence and interest from your audience. So, under all circumstances act confident and enthusiastic. If necessary, *fake* it, but project confidence and interest in your subject.

Speakers are also judged on how well they maintain audience control. Eye contact with the audience is vital; it helps keep attention fixed on you. Lack of eye contact gives the impression you are talking "at" people instead of "to" them. There are a number of tricks for eye contact. The first is strictly physical. You must keep your head from nodding wildly as you glance at your script and back to the audience. To correct this, simply raise the lectern until your head action smooths out. If the lectern is low and you can't change it, step back for enough to allow your eyes to "bounce" off the script into the audience.

If eye contact with everyone in the group is difficult for you, select three or four friendly faces in widely scattered locations. Move your attention from one to another regularly. This will force you to look at *all* sections of the audience. If such direct eye contact is unnerving for you, look at a spot in the center of the forehead of each target person.

Distractions can cause loss of control. Don't permit movement of any kind behind you. That means arranging seating so that you, the speaker—*not* the audience—will be facing the doors and the movement.

Try not to share the stage with anyone. Suggest those near the speaker's stand facing the group move into the audience "so they can see better."

Don't try to compete with noises of any kind. Should an unusual or distracting noise occur *outside* the room, stop . . . comment on the interruption . . . then continue. Do not try to ignore it. (One exception might be a single noise, such as a boom or a backfire; just make sure you are heard, and don't let the interruption interrupt you!)

Depending on protocol, of course, if a side conversation starts in the audience . . . stop . . . look at the offenders (with a smile) until they stop. Then continue. If it happens again, stop again.

"Stage action" movements and breaks in the action emphasize points and help you move smoothly from one subject to another. Silence is a powerful tool. Dramatic pauses ram home ideas. A slightly longer pause, say for a drink of water, can be used to indicate a change of approach. Movement from one side of the podium to the other can have the same effect. For a longer pause or action break, you can move from the lectern to a prop and then change the tempo again by moving back to the lectern.

The skill of knowing how much stage action is correct comes from practicing in front of live audiences, watching the impact, and perfecting the technique. Every presentation then becomes a learning session for you as a speaker. Is this audience manipulation? No way. Keep foremost in your mind that the audience is on your side in desiring a successful presentation.

How About Stage Fright?

Looming in the background is always the specter, "What if, in spite of all this preparation, I bomb? What if I get out there and freeze, get tongue-tied and rooted to the spot? Then a crew of people will have to carry me off the stage, stiff as a board."

Personally, neither of us remembers ever seeing that happen. We have seen some people move with wooden motions and speak with dry mouths—momentarily. Then they loosen up and take control. As we think about it, it seems that the fear of stage fright is more real than stage fright itself.

But, if you have stage fright, you're in good company. Most actors and professional speakers suffer these pangs. Fortunately, there is help. Stage fright can be overcome. A first step is to understand the cause. The second is to put the cause to work for you instead of against you.

Stage fright is an instinct inherited from our earliest ancestors. Nature prepares our bodies for "flight or fright" in a threatening environment. For speakers, the phenomenon lasts only a few moments and leaves. Your body learns that it has functioned and survived without harm; therefore, the preparation for flight or fright is not necessary.

The heightened awareness and stimulation caused by stage fright are actually assets if you react correctly. They can accentuate your animation and appearance of enthusiasm if you let them. Also, if you attempt to mask your fright completely, the audience may think you are bored or lack interest in your subject.

The three steps in controlling stage fright are: (1) *psychological preparation*, (2) *mechanical preparation*, and (3) *physical action*. It may take the entire threefold approach to get this extra surge of energy to work for you.

Psychologically, keep yourself sold on your message: Your presentation is important, it's interesting, it's well prepared, and the audience wants to hear it.

Mechanically, know your material, how you'll deliver it, and how you'll use each prop effectively. Rehearse and make yourself comfortable in the environment of the meeting room. Then rehearse there at least once again. Keeping in mind that stage fright lasts only for a moment, know precisely how to fill that time. One good trick is to memorize, word-for-word, the first couple of paragraphs of your speech; this is a great help in carrying you through that disturbing moment.

Physical action helps dispel stage fright. Before going to the podium, take two or three deep breaths and wet your lips. Arranging it so you walk a few steps to the podium helps too! If the attack strikes while you are actually on the podium, move: get a drink, walk to a prop, or otherwise momentarily distract the audience's attention while you gain composure. If the attack is overwhelming, cause the *audience* to move — call for a 30-second stretch break. You'll regain your cool and keep it during the remainder of your presentation.

Of all these techniques, adequate rehearsal in the environment is probably the most powerful. When it's time to go on, still expect a few butterflies in your stomach. But as one sage said, "The trick is to keep them flying in formation."

Voice Effectiveness

Your voice is a tool for capturing attention and interest. Three basic attributes determine its effectiveness. Your voice should be *audible* (loud enough to be heard and clear enough to be understood). It should be *expressive* enough to be interesting to the listener, and it should be *pleasant* to the ear.

Drama coaches tell us that American voices are often not effective. As a group, we are prone to four major errors in the use of our speaking voices. But the good news is that they also tell us the errors are comparatively *easy* to correct.

The first two errors that drama coaches notice are that we tend to speak *too fast* and *too high*. The third major error has to do with lack of clarity. We tend to be *too lazy* in our pronunciation of words. And coaches say our voices lack expressiveness and sound *too flat*. Let's explain, one by one, the causes and the remedies for these voice errors.

TOO FAST: The major reason for speaking fast is trying to talk as rapidly as we think. As a consequence, we often slur our words, telescope them, or squeeze phrases and thoughts together. The correction, of course, is to speak more slowly — but not too slow. A comfortable word rate for most speakers (and listeners to "live" presenters) ranges from 100 to 125 words per minute.

TOO HIGH: Each of us has a natural pitch and quality of voice, and no two of us sound exactly alike. Yet stress often causes us to force our tone into a higher register than normal. The strain becomes apparent to the audience and reveals our tension. The higher register removes the appearance of warmth and authority, and sometimes adds irritating nasal sounds. When we speak too high, we have little opportunity for the range we need for color, shading, or emphasis.

The obvious correction is to speak lower. Relax the throat muscles and breathe from the diaphragm; this will help you maintain a lower, more normal, confident pitch.

TOO LAZY: Many Americans tend to be jaw-lazy, lip-lazy, and tongue-lazy. As a result, we do not enunciate our words clearly. We "swallow" them.

The remedy is to concentrate on enunciating all of the syllables and all of the consonants. (This has nothing to do with regional accents that add much to our culture.) Clear enunciation can be just as effective with a Southern or Western drawl as with a Midwest twang or an Eastern accent.

TOO FLAT: Americans tend to speak in dull monotones. We often don't use enough emphasis. When we do use it, we sometimes unconsciously emphasize the wrong words or syllables.

The correction is vocal variety. Flexibility in word rate, pitch, and volume— appropriate for the meaning and mood—is very important. A monotone is devoid of emphasis and decreases interest.

In order to achieve vocal variety, work on controlling your breath and listening to yourself.

BREATHING: Breath control is the secret of good voice control. "Collarbone" breathing is something to avoid; it produces shallow tones. Cultivate deep, abdominal breathing. Breathe deeply enough so that you can feel, and even see, your stomach stretch. Take a *deep* breath before reading long phrases or short sentences; then read the *entire* passage before taking another breath.

LISTEN TO YOURSELF AS YOU SPEAK: Radio announcers and singers have a technique for correcting voice range before a performance. They speak or sing while they hold one ear cupped to the head. Try it. With your left hand, push your ear forward, and press it against your head so that it is almost closed. Now, read your material aloud.

Notice that high tones are irritating; lower tones, soothing. Read the material again—cupped ear—and this time keep speaking lower and slower. Repeat this drill until all the voice tones and breath pauses are pleasing to you.

An alternative way some professional speakers use is to stand facing a corner while practicing a speech.

Sold to the Highest Bidder

As said earlier, much of the material in this chapter is excerpted from a workshop Bud Rebedeau conducts. In past years, I (Jim) jointly conducted a number of these workshops entitled "Meeting Dynamics for Speakers." In the workshop, the participants would spend two days working on voice effectiveness and the use of props. On the third day, they would put everything together in a seven- to eight-minute televised presentation.

At one session, we had a person who had been a professional auctioneer—a really good one, as evidenced later. Somewhere along the way this man had traded that profession for his current one of sales manager. At the time of the seminar, only the man himself and I were aware of his auctioneering background.

Since the participants were all sales managers, the charge was for them to select some product and make their most convincing presentation, thus selling the audience on buying the product and the merchandising plan.

On the morning of the televised presentations, we went through four or five speakers before we got to Bob (the former auctioneer). He enthusiastically bounded up onto the stage and flopped down a 24-pound case of coffee onto the lectern. Then he picked up the mike and said:

"The item I have is a 24-pound case of coffee. I'm going to start the bidding at $20." With that, he immediately swung into the universally recognized chant of the auctioneer.

"I gotta 20 dolla and who's going to say 22? Do I hear a 22? Come on ladies and gentlemen, who says 22?"

There was a stunned silence, followed by laughter; then a voice from the back hollered "22 dollars."

"I gotta 22 and who's gonna make it 24, gotta 22 and who's gonna say 24?"

And so the bidding went.

He wound up selling the $60 case of coffee for 82 bucks. His method of presentation hadn't been expected—but it was entertaining! More than that, he knew what he was doing and how to do it well.

Sometimes an offbeat approach can get results, provided you can bring it off. If you don't do it extremely well, though, it's likely to be disastrous. For most of us, the correct approach continues to be improving our scripts, our stage presence, and our voice effectiveness.

Running the Show

When in doubt, win the trick.

— EDMOND HOYLE

Keeping Audience Interest

You know—from experience and perhaps from instinct—how important it is to keep the interest of your audience. No interest, no sale. It's just that simple.

The key to success is *to make the audience a part of the action* whenever you possibly can. The magic word is *participation*. Don't think of yourself as an instructor on one side of a desk, striving valiantly to pound knowledge into the heads of recalcitrant students on the other side. Make sure you put yourself and your audience on the *same* side. Share experiences with the audience that the members can relate to, and do it in such a way that the feeling is always *we*—not *I* and *they*.

The Attention Span

You must never forget that "attention span" is not a term that relates solely to small children. You've probably heard that preschoolers have a relatively short attention span, but you may not have applied the thought to adults.

Well, adults are expected to have a longer attention span than children. However, if you're wise, you won't bank on it too much. Psychologists have learned a great deal about the adult attention span, and they warn us not to expect any miracles. Indeed, their best advice is "Don't try to fool Mother Nature." That's a guaranteed way to lose the battle—*and* the audience. Work *with* nature, not against it.

Figure 11-1 illustrates, very roughly, the way psychologists have charted the adult attention span.

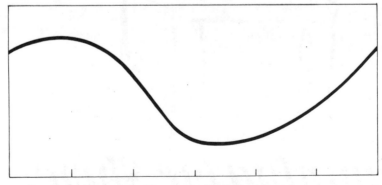

Figure 11-1. Adult attention span chart.

In any given period of, say forty minutes to an hour, you can be sure the audience will give a high level of attention for at least the first ten minutes. That's the nature of the human animal. Partly, it's a matter of curiosity—sizing up what is going on.

But—that first ten-minute period is enormously important. During that time when things are all on your side, if you don't *grab* and *hold* that natural interest, you can lose it almost before you know what's happening.

For the next twenty minutes, the attention curve inevitably starts slanting downward. At first the downturn is relatively slight, but it grows steeper by the minute.

By the end of thirty minutes, the curve finally starts flattening out. At least it does if you are doing a good, professional job.

Now comes the happy moment when the curve reverses direction and starts turning back uphill. The rise is not steep at first, but it should be noticeable—and fairly steady. At the end of about forty minutes, the attention will probably be back somewhere near the high point at which it started.

Again, that's just standard human physiology and psychology. Take advantage of it—don't fight it. The techniques you use or don't use in your presentation can definitely alter the rate of the steepness of the curve; however, no matter how skilled your methods, you can be sure the general changes outlined here are going to take place. So, let's say it one more time: Make sure the opening is a grabber, and, perhaps even more important, *make sure to end each segment on a high note!*

Planning for Participation

Your presentation is not going to be a real success unless you can get your audience involved—and the more involved they are, the better your meeting will be. Not only will the meeting itself have more interest and vitality, but the participants will be much more likely to carry home with them the ideas and concepts that the whole affair was planned to convey in the first place. And, finally, they will continue to remember the really important points long enough to do something about them, instead of simply having a few fuzzy recollections that will not be useful for any practical purpose.

The real difference between the useful participation we are talking about and the "busywork" kind that may give the momentary illusion of success depends primarily on one thing—your ability to direct the discussion and participation tightly along the lines you have previously planned.

Space limitations do not permit a full listing of the many techniques available; accordingly, I'll start with a general list (more or less self-explanatory) and then give you a twelve-step method for directing discussion that I (Jeff) have found useful over the years.

- *Directed writing.* In my "Writing with Precision" seminars, I frequently have the participants do short writing assignments, which are then discussed and criticized, both by me (as the leader) and by the participants.
- *Directed reading.* Okay for variety, but a little of this goes a long way. Don't overdo it.

- *Group discussion.* A really great device for building the feeling of "together-ness" that makes a meeting click.
- *Buzz groups or smaller work groups.* This is a technique used to reach group consensus. I use it frequently in connection with directed writing assignments.
- *Exercises.* Properly designed exercises are among the most effective teaching methods I know of. And frequently I learn something new, or something I hadn't thought of, from the responses of the participants. (Also, I am constantly striving to improve each exercise on the basis of experience; the perfect exercise has yet to be written.)
- *Quizzes.* Giving a quiz, especially unexpectedly, is a good way for you to find out how well your material is going over. Also, after the first "surprise," you can expect participants to be a bit more attentive and alert while they're waiting for another shoe to drop.
- *Experience sharing.* Under tight control, this can be a good technique. Look out that it doesn't become a series of self-aggrandizing "sea stories."
- *Model building and "hands-on" skill practice.* I don't have as much occasion to use these techniques as Jim does. He swears by them.
- *Brainstorming.* One of the best methods I know for coming up with creative ideas and possible solutions to problems.
- *Business games.* This technique is rapidly growing in popularity. Participants usually enjoy it, and it turns their minds toward practical considerations they might otherwise overlook.

Some of the above items work best with small groups, others with larger ones. The best way for you to find what works best is to try them.

A Twelve-Step Checklist

Here is a kind of generalized, something-for-everyone checklist that is designed to get you safely through *most* meetings, large or small:

1. Make an *introductory statement.* In this statement, your purpose is to grab the interest of the audience while the attention curve is at its high point. Start with something familiar—don't get too far out too quickly. Make sure the participants understand what the subject is and why it is important to them. Define any special terms you might have to use. Employ a touch of humor if it comes naturally to you, but don't force it, and don't try to be too clever. Be relaxed, but dignified.

2. *Break the ice* by involving the participants right away. One tried-and-true method is to have the participants stand up and introduce themselves—talk about where they are from, what they do, and tell why they are there and what their expectations are.

   In my "Writing with Precision" seminar, I often begin (after brief introductory remarks) by asking participants to describe a principle that makes for clear writing—for example, "Be concise; don't waste words." This approach reminds students of things they may already know, but perhaps haven't thought about lately, and this sets the stage for moving on to more complex material.

3. *State the topic.* Make sure, each time you begin a new segment (preferably no longer than one hour, to take best advantage of the attention curve), that the topic of discussion is made clear to the participants. One good way is to phrase the topic in the form of a question. Give serious thought about how to phrase the question, for that can make all the difference. Try to put the idea into such a form that it will be thought-provoking and interesting at the same time.

4. *Direct the discussion,* but do it in a low-key, unobtrusive way, without throwing your weight around. Your purpose is to pull together, in useful form, a composite of the experiences and opinions of the participants. Many leaders like to use a flip chart to center the discussion on the pertinent questions—write the topics down on the chart in bold, easy-to-see letters.

5. *Involve each member of the audience,* singly and together. A simple questioning technique will get the ball rolling, and requires no special skill to use. However, you will find your results are much better if you can phrase the questions so that the participants are made aware of how a problem affects them directly—appeal to the "what's-in-it-for-me" angle. If you find some participants are remaining quiet in spite of your best efforts, don't give up. With enough imagination, you should be able to strike a spark.

6. *Steer the discussion.* When the audience begins to participate freely, don't let the discussion get out of control. This is an ever-present danger. If the discussion begins to stray from the subject, it is your job to bring it back, as smoothly and tactfully as you can. (Jim says a good way to handle an offender who is talking too much or going off the track is to walk over to, and stand behind the guilty party.) If necessary, you can take charge by rephrasing the question, then use your answer to regain control of the discussion so you can shift it over to a nontalker or back to the proper topic.

7. *Correct any misunderstandings* as soon as they arise. Don't give them time to take root! You can do this by:

   a. Defining (or redefining) terms or concepts any time a participant appears to be arriving at an interpretation different than the one intended.

   b. Supplying any necessary facts that you may have inadvertently omitted in earlier discussion. Also (more likely to occur), you may suddenly discover that you are aware of factors the group is unaware of, but should know about. Fill in the blanks immediately whenever this situation arises.

c. Restating issues and points under discussion, briefly and clearly. Don't be afraid to do this as many times as necessary if the discussion continues to ramble.

d. Postponing issues that come up too early in the discussion. Be frank with the participants—explain that the issues are not going to be properly understood and discussed until later in the meeting, after more groundwork has been laid and more information is available to the participants.

8. *Question individual members* to encourage full participation by all. Any time you become aware that someone has been sitting for a long time without saying anything, ask that person a direct question. If possible, address the participant by name: "How do you feel about this, Chuck?" *or* "Would you state the point in a different way, Lou?" *or* "How would you answer that question, Susan?"

   The questions I have suggested here are, of course, merely samples. You have thousands of permutations at your disposal, but, in my experience, the most effective ones will be somehow based on the questions that reporters are taught to ask: *who—what—when—where—why—how— how much?*

   Be persistent. Even the shyest participants will thank you for it—later!

9. *Formulate other questions.* I'm a great believer in the organization known as Toastmasters International. One of that organization's many excellent publications, entitled "Conference Leader's Guide," gives some excellent advice on what the booklet calls "key" and "lead" questions. The guide defines "key questions" as those which set the pattern to be followed by indicating the main points to be discussed. "Lead questions" are secondary questions that bring out the answers to key questions, stimulate thought, and promote discussion.

10. *Spotlight other speakers.* I'm a Leo and love holding center stage. Over the years I have learned the hard way that it isn't always a good idea. Avoid temptation and don't save all the good lines for yourself. Your task is to expedite the discussion, and you'll get the best results if you give other speakers the floor from time to time. If you are skillful enough to draw out the shrinking violets of the group, you're a success, no doubt about it.

11. *Be tactful.* If a participant makes remarks you consider totally ridiculous and wrong-headed, keep your opinion to yourself. Don't say: "You jackass—you're totally wrong about this point." Cool it. Say instead, something like "I have a problem accepting that statement in those words," *or* "I don't think I can buy that solution in just that form."

12. *Watch your pacing.* The more accomplished you become as a public speaker, seminar leader, or program chairman, the more you may be tempted to come on "too strong and too long."

   Famed professional speaker Art Fettig reminds us that an audience can get exhausted in a hurry if you don't give them a bit of relief now and then.

In an article entitled "Speaking with Balance" (*Toastmaster* Magazine, September 1975, p. 12), Fettig tells about "one speaker [who] was absolutely great, but within fifteen minutes he had the audience worn out." Then he explains about how he talked with the speaker about timing and pace. Says Fettig: "I suggested he work in a slow vignette along with his other material. He wrote me recently and said he had been studying his entire presentation with his eye on pacing. All through a very important presentation he kept thinking about my advice, and when the audience gave him a standing ovation, he felt it was for both of us."

Okay, folks, with thanks to Toastmasters and various other sources I no longer remember, there are the Twelve Commandments for running a good meeting. Ten were enough for Moses and the Children of Israel, so this might be a good place for me to wind up this chapter.

Telling Your Story with Pictures

The two most engaging powers of an author are to
make new things familiar, and familiar things new.
—SAMUEL JOHNSON

What's Your Message?

When you decide to tell your story with pictures, that's just the beginning. What kind of pictures? It depends on the message and what immediate response you desire from the audience.

Colorful visuals and sound combined with the right words can turn the most pedestrian of meetings into a memorable event. There are a variety of ways to provide both.

Wordy or complicated messages that require study may be best transmitted by using preprinted handouts. These can be further explained by the meeting leader.

Detailed visuals that do not require later referencing can be prime subjects for an overhead projector—with appropriate explanations as needed. (When you use overhead transparencies, you have the added advantage of having a light level high enough for note taking.)

Room lighting needed for slides and motion pictures is a different story. Usually both require low light levels to be effective. We say "usually" because you can employ a rear projection screen and increase the level of light in the meeting room. However, darkness brings out the full value and deep, dense colors that give beauty to slides and movies.

Handouts, lettered charts, transparencies, slides, motion pictures, and closed-circuit television all have their place. Jeff talks about some of those techniques in Chapters 6 to 8. In this chapter, I'm going to zero in on one visual—slides. I've singled them out because they are the most flexible medium for telling stories with pictures. (They're also the most abused visual aid.)

The discussion on slides is to a dual end: (1) to share a few techniques; and (2) to use the development of a slide presentation to branch (in Chapter 14) to the very important topic of *storyboards*.

Which Comes First, the Picture or the Word?

It could be either. Another decision must precede this one. You must determine whether your program is going to be primarily visual, supported by audio—or primarily audio, supported by visuals. The decision made, you can proceed to develop audio and visuals together—either visuals with words as needed, or words with visuals as needed—unfolding side by side as your story takes shape.

In this chapter, we'll begin by taking a simple written story and showing you the first steps in how a printed article can be transformed into a visualized program. We'll show you the preliminary steps in shifting from materials to be *read* to materials to be *seen and heard*. Then, in the next chapters, we'll show you how to put it all together with storyboards. Following that will come a few tips on how to dress up a slide presentation. From there, we'll briefly branch out to discuss multiple-screen presentations.

Storyboards Help Keep Your Thoughts Straight

Storyboards are one of the essentials in preparing a story that is going to be told visually. They keep your thoughts straight; they give you the options of easily shifting material around; and, most important, they offer you an ideal means of showing your work-in-progress to others. The last point is vital when you're writing for someone else. And even if you have full control over the end product, it can be useful if you want other opinions before you proceed to the development of costly finished art.

Trying to tell someone how a visual presentation works without having the pictures is like describing the Mona Lisa as a picture of a woman with a funny smile. The easiest way of overviewing an audiovisual presentation is with storyboards in hand. Then, as you show and tell simultaneously, your listeners can easily tune in on the same wave length as you. When you say "dog," they know you mean a cocker spaniel—not a great dane, a miniature poodle, or a collie. In this way, misunderstandings are avoided entirely or corrected well in advance of producing the finished product.

Since storyboards are so important, why doesn't everyone use them? Either they don't know how or they don't realize how much time they can save by using them. Until people get used to using storyboards, they tend to feel that they are just having to do a lot of extra work. In reality, they are getting their act together in the quickest and most efficient way. That means they are turning the written word into a pleasing, effective communication device—one that appeals to more than just one sense.

Story into Pictures—the First Step

As a practical application of what Jim is talking about, let's develop a very simple little story into a slide presentation. The story is about housing and household energy requirements. In real life, the writer would take the thrust of the article and generate a sound/slide or motion picture film.

Here, rather than do that in one fell swoop, we're going to carry you through four different presentations. With each, we'll alter the words slightly and shift the balance between them and the visuals. For a good reason, too. We want to show how your writing will change as your skill at writing words to be *spoken* evolves.

Here's the basic story:

BACK TO THE CAVE?

The story of housing is the same as the story of man; down through the ages they have evolved together. With each evolution, shelters changed to meet man's needs and to employ the materials at hand. In the past, with abundant resources, we were able to do this with very little regard to the long-range effect. Today we know better. So, the current question is, Where do we go next?

To fully understand the evolutionary crisis, we have to go back to the beginning. Housing on our continent probably began with simple lean-tos or, where they were available, caves. The first change occurred when some of the hunters became agrarians. The travel distance between the caves and their crops became impractical, and their solution was to build houses close to their work, which enabled them to guard their fields. They used readily available materials—sticks, mud, and rocks.

As man's implements changed from stone to steel, man was able to use larger timber and other materials. What he chose depended on the need for or lack of mobility. The nomadic tribes turned to temporary or portable shelters constructed of hide, reeds, and poles. The farmers continued using stone, but were able to add clay and/or large timbers.

After centuries of evolution, all men wound up with houses that were just about alike. They were boxlike structures with glass windows and doors on hinges—wooden or brick-veneer walls and a shingled roof. With the advent of the energy crisis, man plunged deeper into modern technology, or turned back to renew his acquaintance with building materials of the past.

As a result, housing is beginning to become more varied. Those on the path of advanced technology are adding extra layers of glass, foam, and other forms of insulation, and weather stripping. And, although their houses may externally look the same, they are more energy-efficient. On the other hand, there are people who advocate the "back-to-the-earth" movement. These people are employing designs and materials from all the past centuries.

Both groups have the same things in mind: conserve what energy we now have and look for alternative ways to generate more. Some energy requirements are being met through once again harnessing nature's resources: water, wind, and the sun. Other requirements are being met through fermenting grain for alcohol. But we could also ferment other materials such as garbage, compost, and manure.

Cleaning up the environment is only a part of the issue. The bigger issue is how to use and reuse renewable forms of energy.

Currently available are a number of home systems that utilize a variety of these methods or materials . . .

Not a bad story for print. It's also pretty typical of the neutral style of writing many people use when writing this type of material. Jim purposely chose this because, while not totally colorless, it is fairly neutral. Also, it's a topical subject, but not one most of us would need or choose for a business presentation.

A first step toward adapting this story to a slide presentation (within Jim's frame of reference) might look something like this:

The story of housing is the same as the story of man. Down through the ages they have evolved together. With each evolution of man, shelters changed to meet his needs and to employ the materials at hand. In the past, with abundant resources, man was able to do this with little regard to the long-range effect.

WHERE DO WE GO NEXT ?

The current question is, Where do we go next? To fully understand this evolutionary crisis, we have to go back to the beginning.

Housing on our continent, so I'm told, began with caves. The first change occurred when some of the hunters became agrarians. They built houses close to their work so they could guard their fields. For them, caves were out—and sticks, mud, and rocks were in. As man's implements changed from stone to steel, man was able to use larger timber and other materials. What he chose depended on his need for or lack of mobility.

The nomadic tribes turned to temporary or portable shelters—hide, reeds, and poles. The farmers continued using stone, but they were able to add clay and/or large timber.

After centuries of evolution, all men wound up with houses that were just about alike—designed like cubes or a series of cubes with glass or wood covering the openings in the wall.

That was until the advent of the energy crisis, when man plunged deeper into modern technology, or turned back . . . to renew his acquaintance with building materials of the past.

As a result, housing is beginning to become more varied. Those on the path of advanced technology are adding extra layers of glass, foam, and other forms of insulation, and weather stripping. And, although their houses may externally look the same, they are more energy-efficient. On the other hand, there are those who advocate the "back-to-the-earth" movement. These people are employing designs and materials from all the past centuries.

Both groups have the same things in mind: conserve what energy we now have and look for alternate ways to generate more. Some energy requirements are being met through once again harnessing nature's resources—water, wind, and the sun. Other requirements are being met through fermenting grain to make alcohol. But we could also ferment other materials such as garbage, compost, and manure.

WATER WIND SUN

Cleaning up the environment is only a part of the issue. The bigger issue is how to use and reuse renewable forms of energy.

Let's look at some home systems that utilize a variety of these methods or materials . . .

Figure 12-1. Back to the cave (example 2).

As Jim said before presenting this script, it would be typical of what we see people do. Essentially, what has happened is that a few words were edited, and every so often a slide was thrown in. Even though the script is typical, it has problems. The main one is that we often forget *spoken English differs from written text*. Also, in our effort to be understood, we tend to verbalize more than necessary. Too often, we back up this (please excuse this polysyllabic monstrosity) *oververbalization* with more words on slides.

Too few slides—and too many of those few devoted to words. This is not a unique situation. Typically, people who are unaccustomed to working with visuals place too much emphasis on the value of the word. Consequently, in addition to *saying* it, they want to show it *written out on the screen*. (Occasionally, in training scripts, this is a worthwhile thing to do. In programs devoted to general information, however, we urge that you try to avoid that technique.)

The other thing novices have a tendency to do is to hold each slide on the screen until they feel they get their money's worth from it. No question about it, slides do cost money. And you can rationalize that the scripting (if you're doing it yourself) is only a matter of time. But, as you'll see in the next chapter, well-balanced programs need visuals as well as narration.

Okay, please bear this background information in mind as we set forth the step-by-step procedures in putting together a storyboard presentation that really works.

Turning Words and Pictures Into a Polished Slide Presentation

True eloquence consists in saying all that should be,
not all that could be said.
— FRANCOIS, DUC DE LAROCHEFOUCAULD

Get Out the Scissors

In the previous chapter, we introduced you to the basic technique of putting pictures to words (as it is most often practiced). Now we are going to take you step-by-step as we shape the original rough version into a polished slide presentation. Here goes:

Working from the version we had achieved in Figure 12-1, let's do three quick things to the script to improve it. First, we'll add a title slide and do some minor editing as we read our script aloud. Next—and this is very important—we'll *put the slide changes within the text instead of at the head of each paragraph*. The dots will be placed to allow 9/10ths of a second between pushing the button and the time when the slide appears on the screen.

Remember, the black dot indicates when the button is pushed for a slide change. It actually appears about two words later.

BACK TO THE CAVE?

BACK TO THE CAVE ?

•

The story of man and shelter are the same. Down through the ages they have evolved together. With each evolution of man, shelter changed to meet his needs. And, to employ the materials at hand.

In the past, with abundant natural resources, man was able to do this . . . with little regard to long-range effect. The ● question is, Where do we go next?

To fully understand that, we have to go back to the beginning.

The first house on our continent was probably a lean-to ● or a cave. The move away from the cave began when some of the hunters became farmers. They built houses close to their work so they could guard their fields. For them, caves were out, and sticks, mud, and rocks were in. As man's implements changed from stone to steel, man was able to use larger timber and other materials. What he chose depended on his need for or lack of mobility.

The nomadic tribes turned to temporary or portable shelters. Hide. Reeds. And poles. The farmers continued using stone . . . but they were able to add clay and/or large timber.

After centuries of evolution, all men wound up with houses just about alike. Designed ● like cubes or a series of cubes with glass or wood covering the openings in the walls.

That was until the advent of the energy crisis, when man plunged deeper into modern technology, or turned back . . . to renew his acquaintance with building materials of the past.

As a result, housing is becoming more varied: Those on the path of advanced technology are adding extra layers of glass, foam, and other forms of insulation, and weather stripping. And, although their houses may externally look the same, they are more energy efficient. On the other hand, we have the back-to-the-earth movement. These people are employing designs and materials from all ● of the past centuries.

Both groups have the same thing in mind: conserve what energy we now have . . . and . . . look for alternate ways to generate more. Some energy requirements are being met through once again harnessing nature's resources—water, wind, and the sun. Other requirements are being met through fermenting grain. But, we could also ferment other materials such as garbage, compost, and manure.

Cleaning up the environment is only a part of the issue. The bigger issue is how to use and reuse renewable forms of energy.

Let's look at some home systems that utilize a variety of these methods or materials . . .

Figure 13-1. Back to the cave (example 3).

Remember—the pulsing dots (●) precede the actual dropping of the slide by approximately ⁹⁄₁₀ of a second.

This version was better, but it's a long way from good. There are still too many words, some stilted language, and it's crying for more pictures. So our next step is to tighten up the words, spread them out—and carry more of the story with our visuals.

If you can bear with us, we'll try the same story one more time. But, this time our chief concern will be to retain the thrust of the story—not every phrase—and visually capture the audience. If you remember our earlier comments on learning retention, this further balancing of words and visuals makes a lot of sense.

Before we start, keep one thing in mind. Scripts for the spoken word don't always look good on paper. Also, we've spread them out to provide pacing. It'll help to read the script aloud—or at least, if no one is watching you, move your lips as you read this script.

BACK TO THE CAVE?

●

BACK
TO THE
CAVE ?

Man and shelter . . . •

Evolving together . . . •

down through the ages . . . •

• Each adapting to the other . . . to fit man's needs . . .

• and the materials at hand . . .

But, in time all houses begin to look alike. . . . cubes.

. . . or for the rich, a series of cubes.

With glass, or wood covering the openings.

There was no regard for the future impact of these energy drains . . .

That was until now! Suddenly everybody's concerned.

Energy and natural resources that were once abundant are almost unaffordable.

People are becoming singled-minded.

Their thoughts—
Conserve energy and develop alternate ways of generating more.

The answer for some is to plunge deeper and faster into modern technology to improve on their cubes.

Others are looking back toward older proven methods.

Some are using the earth for homes.

•

Dealing directly with the elements and harnessing nature's forces on an individual basis.

•

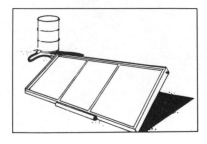

Some other energy options are coal, oil, or alcohol production.

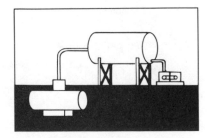

Possibilities for the future include fermenting:
manure,
garbage,
and compost.

•Preserving natural resources and cleaning up the environment are only a part of the picture.

The real issue is using. . .

Modifying
• and
reusing renewable sources of energy.

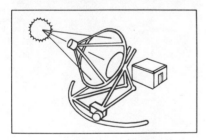

•

Let's look at some home systems that do that . . . (and so on).

Figure 13-2. Back to the cave (example 4).

Let's see what we've done in this final surgery. The presentation looks longer, because we've used more paper. In reality, it will fit into about the same amount of time as that required by the first visualized script. And, even though we used more visuals, we reduced the number of words from 455 to fewer than 200. The words that were removed weren't necessary to maintain the thrust of the script. In fact, this was a case of words getting in the way of the message.

Once you're at this stage in a script, you can branch off in several directions. For instance, if this script is intended to be narrated on audio tape, it could be turned into a self-sustaining mechanized program. If that is what you want to do, you need a narrator; you also need a means for "pulsing" the tape so it triggers a slide projector. If the presentation is to be made live, which is usually the best way, you need to make sure you have the pulsing points at the correct places on the script. Of course, there is the consideration (which is usually made earlier in the game) as to whether your presentation should be a single-, double-, or triple-screen presentation.

In the next chapter, we'll cover the mechanics of putting an A/V presentation together, narration, and other related details. Then, in a later chapter, we'll give a brief overview of multiscreen, multimedia, or multi-image techniques. An in-depth coverage of this subject would almost be a book in itself.

Maybe one of these days . . .

Using Storyboards to Build a Smooth Presentation

*Not that the story need be long, but it will take a
long while to make it short.*

           —HENRY DAVID THOREAU

Making Your Creative Thinking Easily Understood

It's been said that matching visuals to words or vice versa is one of the truly great art forms. That may be true or it may not be—but that's only the creative side of the story. The other side is all of the mechanical plans and techniques that prepare the words and pictures for maximum impact. But before we leave the creative process behind, I want to offer a final thought. All people are creative; it just varies in form from individual to individual.

Creative efforts begin to pay off when they are controlled and put into an easily understood format that can be shared by others. In A/V productions, the first step in that direction is with storyboards.

Storyboards

Simply stated, storyboards are the result of combining words and visuals on a piece of paper. Then why call them boards? Because at some point they're usually drawn or pasted onto art board. That's the same stuff some people call pasteboard. That's done so they can be handled without becoming dog-eared.

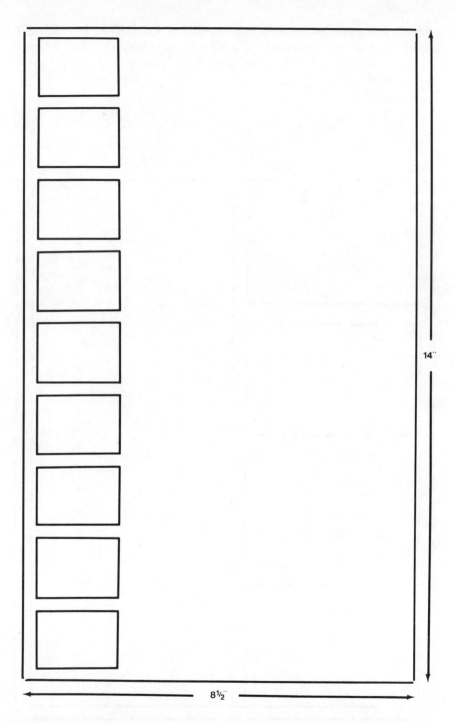

Figure 14-1. Format paper for A/V scripting. This is the same format paper we used in our housing script.

Storyboards can come in an infinite number of sizes and configurations. It depends on their use. For instance, I personally use different sizes for different scripts. And, sometimes I change sizes as I advance through the various stages of the same script.

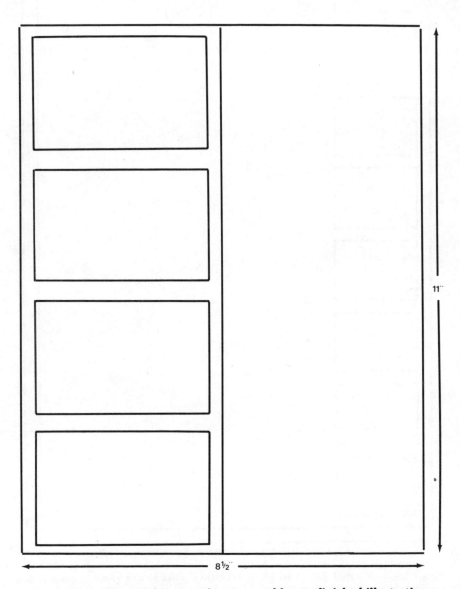

Figure 14-2. We use this size when we need larger finished illustrations.

In this chapter, we'll zero in on the single-screen format paper we used earlier and one-size individual storyboard, and the practicalities of putting them to use.

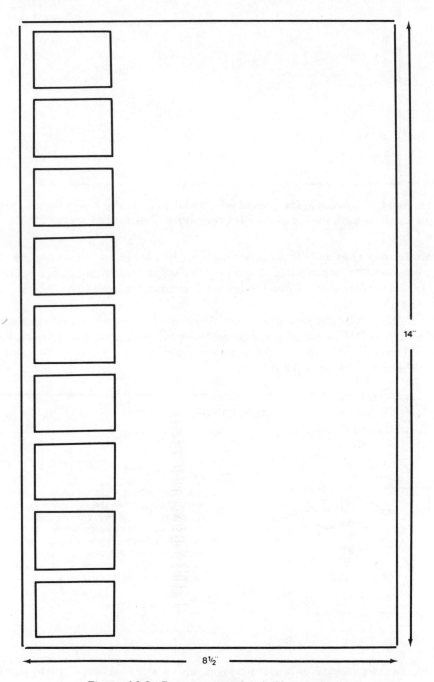

Figure 14-3. Format paper for A/V scripting.

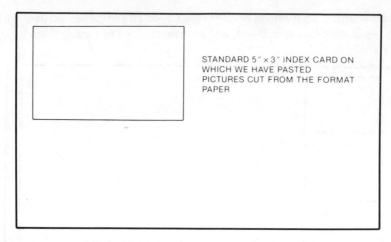

STANDARD 5″ × 3″ INDEX CARD ON
WHICH WE HAVE PASTED
PICTURES CUT FROM THE FORMAT
PAPER

Figure 14-4. Individual storyboard using standard 5-inch by 3-inch index cards on which we have pasted picture frames cut from the format paper.

Single-screen format. For discussion purposes, let's revisit the housing script and go over how it was generated. (I know this one script must be getting boring, but look at the bright side—it won't distract your attention from the techniques we're offering.)

We began the script on format paper. As I wrote, I put a single thought passage opposite each block on the paper. Immediately before or after that, I roughly— and I mean roughly—sketched a picture or designation.

That went something like this:

BACK TO THE CAVE?

The story of housing is the same as the story of man. Down through the ages they have evolved together. With each evolution of man, shelters changed to meet his needs and to employ the materials at hand. In the past, with abundant resources at hand, man was able to do this with little regard to the long-range effect.

Figure 14-5. Single thought passages are written opposite each rough drawing.

The current question is, Where do we go next? To fully understand this evolutionary crisis, we have to go back to the beginning.

Housing on our continent, so I'm told, began with caves. The first change occurred when some of the hunters became agrarians. They built houses close to their work so they could guard their fields. For them, caves were out, and sticks, mud, and rocks were in. As man's implements changed from stone to steel, man was able to use larger timber and other materials. What he chose depended on his need for or lack of mobility.

You'll notice that when I couldn't quickly bring to mind an image of a cave and cave dweller, I merely wrote in the words and kept going. No sweat. Missing sketches can be roughed in during the next step. The main idea is to keep going until the basics of the script are on paper.

After I was satisfied that the pictures and words basically went together, I switched over to the individual storyboards.

Individual storyboards. As I transferred the copy to individual storyboards, I refined it and improved the drawings. I also double-checked that the visual was correct for the copy at that stage. An individual card looked like this:

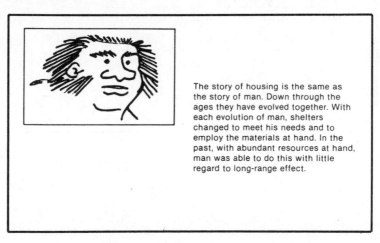

The story of housing is the same as the story of man. Down through the ages they have evolved together. With each evolution of man, shelters changed to meet his needs and to employ the materials at hand. In the past, with abundant resources at hand, man was able to do this with little regard to long-range effect.

Figure 14-6. Individual storyboard.

The cards were then sequentially numbered. When you do this, the number of cards in the stack is equal to the number of visuals you intend to use.

Display Boards

How you handle the stack of cards depends on how often you're going to write these types of scripts. If it's once a year, merely spread the cards out on a large flat surface—a tabletop for instance. Or, you may wish to tack them on the wall with push pins.

If you're going to have a continuing use for it, I suggest you buy or construct a wall-mounted display board. They're hard to find in stores, but are relatively easy and inexpensive to make. I have done both—bought and made display boards. The most recent ones I bought were extruded plastic backed with clear plastic strips. I bought them through Metro Educational Products, P. O. Box 8463, Rochester, New York 14618.

2" CLEAR PLASTIC STRIPS

Figure 14-7. A display board for individual storyboards.

The ones I made in the past were faced with clear plastic strips stapled or glued at the bottom of each so they formed continuous pockets the width of the board. The edges were taped down on solid backs made from art board (but plastic or very thin plywood would work as well).

Either type of board, bought or homemade, works the same way. The cards are arranged in sequentially vertical rows in the pockets.

1	6	11	16
2	7	12	17
3	8	13	etc.
4	9	14	
5	10	15	

Once this is done, the cards are put up on the wall with all of them visible. When you can see them all at once, you'll begin to see the rhythm of the finished piece. For example, you'll see that in certain parts of the script, the copy far outweighs the visuals. Or, you may see that you have too many quick visual cuts in a row that can give the effect of a ping-pong match. Either way, you'll want to make some adjustments to smooth out the rhythm of the slides and the words. Beware, though, of the trap of setting a highly stylized rhythm. If you become too predictable, you'll lose the elements of surprise and discovery. (That's another way of saying you'll bore your audience.) What you're looking for is a nice flow and a good mix between long verbal passages and quick slide changes.

Next, you'll be looking at the sequence of cards. The little story we did earlier is chronological in nature, so sequencing was minimal, but there were a couple of misplaced passages. When that happens, it's a simple matter to pull the misplaced storyboard and reinsert it in a better place in the sequence.

What next? The picture and the verbal passage that don't quite mesh. If a certain visual would fit better with a different piece of copy, that's also simple to fix. Cut the picture off the card and tape it to one with copy that fits better. (Incidentally, I did that in four places during the final draft of our earlier story.) Pictures or copy blocks that are just plain wrong are also simple to fix. Do it the same way—write or draw what you like better and paste it over the offending copy or picture.

Right there on the wall you've just done most of the real editing. Continuity, rhythm, balance between copy and picture, and the relationship of copy to visuals have all been ironed out.

So now that's all done. What's the next step? That depends on you. If you need approval from other persons, you might show them the program right there on the wall. If the visuals are to be photographs of people or scenes, you have the shot list for the photographer. If you are going to use art-type visuals, you have the sketches you need to discuss finished slides with an artist. But before we go any further, let's go over a point I glossed over earlier— refining your sketches.

You may have enough natural ability to do that with no problem. And, of course, if you don't need to show or discuss your program with others, a very rough sketch will do. For instance, stick figures for people, written words for more complex visuals, and so on.

Now that we have a basic program put together, let's add some sparkle. How far you want to go is up to you, but at the very least, you want to time your slides to drop at the proper second for maximum effectiveness. After we discuss how that's done, we'll talk about some ways to make your presentation glisten.

Getting Your A/V Act Together Mechanically

It has long been an axiom of mine that little things
are infinitely the most important.

— SIR ARTHUR CONAN DOYLE

"Fine-Tuning" Techniques

Much of the success of an A/V program is built in through the almost mechanical detail employed in its preparation and presentation.

Storyboards were a good example of mechanics being used to aid creative efforts. But that's only one of many needed techniques. In this chapter we'll acquaint you with some of the other methods of displaying your professionalism.

Some people might liken these techniques to creativity, but to others it's pure and simple mechanical detail. But by whatever name they're called, these techniques, when polished, are enough to turn a humdrum slide presentation into a professional production or make an already good production glisten.

Dressing Up the Slide Presentation

A few touches here and there can add sparkle to your visual presentation. The earlier in your planning you begin, the more you can build in. The first place that requires your attention is format. And, of course, the quality of your slides will determine the quality of the finished product. How you begin and end your presentation and how smooth slide changes and any necessary tray changes are made are the icing on the cake. We'll take these topics in order, give an overview of mechanically operated presentations, and then talk about where you can go from there.

Format. Try not to mix vertical format slides with horizontal ones and don't mix super slides with either. Choose one format and stick with it. Generally, that will be the regular horizontal format. Everything seems to work better in that format. For instance, you can roll your screen up or down, whichever the case may be, so the projected slide completely fills the screen. (When slides don't completely fill the screen, the white unfilled portions become distracting to your audience.) It's also possible to fit vertical formats on a fully extended screen. The problem is that an entire program, unless of very specialized material, isn't as interesting.

A basic mechanical rule in making slides is that the art be made in proportion to their projected size. Usually that's 3 x 2 units. One way artists keep everything in this format is to make a little cardboard frame larger but in correct ratio to a slide. With the frame, they draw faint borders around the intended viewing area of their layouts and put all of the art inside the borders. If you do this, be sure to get the border lines off before the art is photographed. Another way, of course, is to cut the layout paper into correct format ratios. I've heard artists discuss the pros and cons of each method, but it looks like a dealer's choice to me.

It's extremely distracting if projected slides bleed off the top, bottom, or sides of the screen. That means, in addition to correct format, you need the right size screen, the right length of throw from projector to screen, and the right length lens. The measurement charts put out by the Kodak Company are excellent for focal lengths, throw distances, and screen sizes, but you will still need to make the final adjustments so the screen is completely filled.

Quality of Slides. Resist the temptation to type a message and photograph it to make a slide. Use symbols wherever possible. If you absolutely need a portion of your message in words, use dry-transfer letters (Prestype™, Letraget™, etc.) or set type and put the message in as few words as possible.

The technical difficulty in using words from a typewriter is they visually break up on the screen. Typewriters have a way of making some characters lighter or darker or blurred on the edges. In a letter or other typed document, their shifts in density or clarity are imperceptible. Not so though when each individual letter is projected twenty more times its normal size. A new Selectric™ with a clean element can reduce this problem, but it can't cure it. We'll be talking more about preparation of slides in later chapters.

Reducing light flashes. You've more than likely seen a number of slide presentations in which the first and last thing you saw was the screen filled with direct unfiltered light from the projector. That's a pet peeve of many people. Me included. At the end of the presentation, this light flash can be almost blinding. At best, it's damn annoying. Getting rid of these flashes can help make you look like a pro.

Here are some of the tricks pros use. The first and most common is to put blank, opaque slides at heads and tails of presentations. Your film processor can make a few of these for you. They usually use the ends off of processed film rolls. It's merely a process of putting a scrap of that in a slide mount. This casts a dark outline onto the screen but it keeps the light from blinding your audience. Some other alternatives are to project a light wash onto the screen. Wash slides are made by mounting a piece of colored gel (transparent colored plastic) in a slide mount.

One other device professionals use are pieces of art board cut to the appropriate size. They place them in first and last positions of the program—green in the first hole, and red at the end. The opaque art board will not transmit light from the projector, but it will cause a small light spill at the top. This allows you to turn the projector on in advance of the meeting. Then, in a semidarkened room, the red- or green-tinged light spill lets you know the position of the tray. Green equals "ready to run" and red means "hold right here or you're going to get a flash of light on the screen." And, by holding the tray on the red opaque, you can switch the projector off at your leisure. Somehow, it just adds a little class to your act by not clambering back and forth across the room to fire up or kill the projector.

Which also brings us to another point. During the live slide presentation, who controls the projector, you the speaker, or an assistant?

Who pushes the button? Both speakers and audiences can be distracted if the meeting leader is the one who is pushing the button for the slide projector. We won't say it should *never* be done. In small get-togethers where informality is the rule and you wish to do some ad-libbing, then you hold the "pickle switch." But in more formal presentations, get someone else to control the visuals.

Generally, when someone else is controlling the visuals, the operator is located near the projector, right on the spot in case mechanical problems develop.

To make sure everything else goes right, two more precautions are in order. First, make sure the projectionist has a cued script. Second, make sure the presenter sticks to the script! (*Note*: Murphy's Law guarantees that the projectionist won't have enough light to read the script. Furnish a 15-watt reading lamp, or at least a penlight. As a last precaution, tape the switch down to a tabletop or other hard surface so it doesn't get lost in the dark.)

If you are a speaker and someone else is pushing the button, there are a couple of things you can do to add to your professionalism. The first is to refrain from asking the operator to turn the projector on or off or to push the button. A better idea is to arrange a visual signal to give the cue when you're ready for the program to start. You will probably want to arrange at least one more signal that means punch the button. (You could consider a final signal that says, "Read the script, you big dummy. You're lost!")

Another thing you'll want to do as a speaker is to avoid looking openly at the screen. The visuals are there for the audience. Trust your assistant to get the right picture up there at the right time. The only exception to this is when you need to refer specifically to something that is happening on the screen.

Let us remind you one more time of this most important point: *Stick to the script!* The button doesn't get pushed until you say the right words.

Timing slides to drop. You can read the scripts, estimate where the button should be pushed, and put a pulsing dot on the script as we did earlier. That's all right and will usually work out on simple presentations. But there are some programs that can be greatly enhanced if the slide falls exactly at a given time—no microsecond variation one way or the other. This takes a little playing around with the script and the projector or projectors and the slides. There will be a couple of other situations in which you'll be able to use the technique I am about to offer. The first situation is when you're still not sure if you have the right number of slides for the words or vice versa; the second situation is when you want some consultation on the flow of the program before you go to the expense of getting the finished slides made. What you can do to cover yourself in these situations is to hand-make some temporary throw-away slides. You can arrange and rearrange these and the pulsing dots until you get your program honed and the finished slides in hand. Then, it's an easy matter to replace the throw-aways with the pretty stuff.

Temporary Handmade Slides

Blank slides with a film surface suitable to letter or draw on can be purchased. There are several different brands of these. You can rough-sketch or letter a full set of these quickly, put them in the projector, read your message aloud, and click away. This will give you a pretty good idea of how everything fits together and flows.

One brand of blank slides I use is "u" slides. These can be purchased in boxes of eighty at a fairly nominal cost. You can mail order them through: Visual Horizons, Rochester, New York.

Whether you buy "u" slides or another brand, you need a writing instrument that will work on them. Regular inks have a way of curdling or fading out when they are exposed to the heat of a projection bulb. If there is a convenient full-line art supply store near you, discuss the problem with a salesperson and get recommendations for the correct pens. In addition to ink, there are some leads for mechanical pencils that can be successfully used on film stock.

Buying Slides

Sometimes the most prudent method of acquiring slides is to buy them. This may seem like a switch on my part—considering the amount of text devoted to making slides. It really isn't. The guts of a sound/slide show is the match between words and visuals. For the sake of finances or art, that means occasionally buying someone else's work. The type of slides you might consider buying fall into five broad categories:

1. Generic instructions
2. Universal symbols
3. Generic backgrounds
4. Civic or municipal scenes
5. The absolutely correct scene or glamour shot

Generic instruction slides are those that say "coffee break," "work session," "the end," and so on. There are a number of companies that produce and sell, by mail order, this type of slide. Usually they are bought in sets of eight to ten assorted titles at a cost of $20 to $25. Many of these companies advertise in the meeting and training professional magazines. If you're interested in these, check the small ads in the professional journals.

Universal symbols are in memory storage at the companies that generate computer-based slides. These companies usually have a showroom and/or a catalog from which to choose symbols, typefaces, and words. You pick out what you want, and they combine it via the computer to produce a finished slide. Some of these companies have an option of putting your finished slide compositions in storage under your name. At future dates you can draw from that storage as well as their general library. If you wish, you can compose an entire slide show in this manner. The advantage is high-quality slides. The disadvantages are the limitations of the computer and *sometimes* cost.

The best-known name in that business is Genographics, a division of General Electric. However, they are not the only company in the business. If you live in a major metropolitan area, you will find other suppliers listed in the Yellow Pages of the telephone directory.

Generic backgrounds, as referred to here, are scenic shots of a specific item. Mountains, apple orchards, orange groves, and corn fields all fall into this category. You may wish to show something similar in a program, but not have access to the scene. Don't despair. Most agricultural commodities have state or national associations. They usually have slide libraries and may, at a nominal cost, sell you a set of duplicate slides.

In your public library you will be able to locate a *National Guide to Associations.* It contains the mailing addresses and telephone numbers of thousands of associations. Pick the one that sounds most likely for your purposes and drop them a letter.

Civic and municipal scenes are standard fare at most chambers of commerce and local tourist bureaus. Some area gift shops also deal in local scenes. The charge is usually nominal for slides bought this way.

The absolutely correct shot may be next to impossible for you to get (at least within a budget). If you find yourself in that situation, you can try a stock photo house. There you can either rent or buy the perfect slide. As an example, recently I needed a beautiful sunrise of a particular composition. In itself, that doesn't sound like a big deal — but it was. I had a certain effect in mind — and didn't find it in the one hundred or so sunrise shots on hand. At that point, I turned to a stock photo house. Here in Houston, there are a number of stock photo houses, each specializing in a certain category: glamour art, outdoor scenery, retail customers shopping, and so forth. Locating by phone the one that seemed to have the most variety in this category, I visited the showroom. On hand were several hundred sunrise and sunset shots — including the one I had in mind. It cost me 80 bucks. That's a lot of money, but only a fraction of what it could have cost to hire a photographer and hope I got what I wanted. I don't recommend stock photo houses as a frequent option, but on occasion they're worth investigating and using.

It seems that throughout this book we wind up sections such as this with one last word of caution. Not wishing to break that pattern, here is your word of caution about buying slides: *Regardless of how expensive or inexpensive purchased slides are, they must meet all of the standards for clarity, legibility, and compatibility with the other slides in the presentation.*

Dropping Slides

There are only eight ways to load a slide into a carousel tray. Sometimes when I'm fumbling around, it seems like there are more. Considering I've handled hundreds of thousands of slides during my career, it's stupid to fumble around at all. That just happens to be one of my major hangups — getting them in right the first time around.

I think part of the problem is that it's too simple. Consequently, I don't always think of the one proper way to load slides right off the bat. Even though the procedure is so simple it hurts your head, I'm including this bit for all of the other absent-minded meeting leaders.

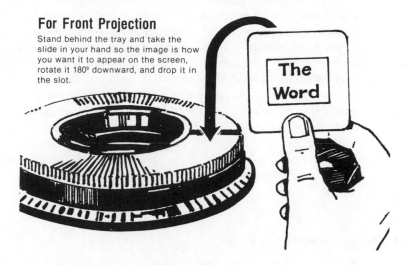

For Front Projection

Stand behind the tray and take the slide in your hand so the image is how you want it to appear on the screen, rotate it 180° downward, and drop it in the slot.

The Word

Figure 15-1. Loading a slide tray for front projection.

For Rear Projection

Rotate the slide so the image is backwards

LIKE THIS

The Word

Then, rotate the slide 180° downward and drop it in the slot.

Figure 15-2. Loading a slide tray for rear projection.

After you have the slides in the tray, put the locking ring on the tray. It just isn't any fun picking spilled slides up from the floor and resorting them because a tray was accidentally knocked over.

Forgive me if you think these procedures are too simple to talk about, but I know there are other people as absent-minded as I am.

One of the most famous of these absent-minded people I've heard about was a brilliant World War II naval commander. Every day upon taking the bridge, he would take a gold key from his pocket, open a small mahogany chest, read the message contained there, replace it, and relock the chest. After this, he put his vessel through the most intricate of maneuvers. He never lost a fight or blew a mission. Years later and upon his retirement, curiosity got the best of one of his six sailing mates. "Captain, I've sailed the seven seas with you for close to thirty years, and day-by-day you read the same message. What is it—a secret motto, prayer, or what?" Without a word, the captain took the gold key, opened the chest and handed the slip of paper over. Here was the whole message: "Port is left and starboard is right."

So, for those of you who aren't forgetful, my apologies. For the others—here it is—just tear this page from the book, buy yourself a small mahogany chest, a gold key . . .

81 Slides in an 80-Slide Tray

Sounds silly but it happens, and there are a couple of good cases for it. The first is obvious—somebody miscounted or added one slide more than you have slots for in the tray. The other case is when you have a lot more than 80 slides and you need to put them in two or more trays. You need something to keep the screen filled while you are changing trays.

That's your eighty-first slide. The way it works is to put your eighty-first slide into the projector before you mount tray No. 1. Then, when the tray is mounted and set on "0," push the release lever so it lifts the slide into that upside down slot under "0." Then, advance the tray to slot No. 1. The eighty-first slide is trapped under "0" but will fall as number 81. When it's time to change trays, you're on "0" so the tray isn't locked down. That makes it simple. Just lift tray No. 1 off and slap the next one on. When you punch the next slide, No. 81 goes up into the "0" hole on that tray and you're off and running again.

You might be asking about now why I'm not suggesting the seemingly easier alternative of using a 140-slot slide tray. Simple reason—I don't trust them. In fact, there is only one type of tray I trust, and that's the gray Ektagraphic 80-slot tray. The 140-count trays really only function with paper mounted slides. For professional purposes, we usually use plastic mounts for the weight and occasionally even glass mounts. Paper mounts, because they are light in weight, don't always positively drop. Sometimes they warp or bend a little. A crimped slide and the narrow slot on a 140-count tray are an invitation for potential problems. A hung slide in the middle of a presentation just isn't fun.

One last word before we leave the topic of slide trays: After you get the gray Ektagraphic slide tray, attach it to an Ektagraphic projector. Year in and year out for dependable operation and clear projection, they're number one in my book.

Mechanically Operated Programs

On occasion, you'll have the need to mix mechanically operated sound/slide presentations with live ones. That can make a good mix. If they're done right, they can add a lot to your presentation. At other times, say at a convention booth, they're a necessity. Single-projector mechanical programs are put together just like the program we developed earlier—up to a point. That point is the narration or audio track.

If you can swing it budgetwise, get a professional voice for the narration. Two big reasons: The fact is that when you get into the area of mechanical programs, you, in a way, are competing with all other mechanical reproductions—namely, television and movies. You may not have thought of it that way before, but that's just one of the psychological shifts that an audience makes in their minds. The second reason is the quality of the voice. Unless you have had extensive training, it's next to impossible to have the clarity and emphasis that professionals possess.

This may be new ground for you, but don't get into a panic about producing a mechanically controlled presentation. The only new things about it are hiring a voice talent and renting a studio. If you have never done this before, begin by getting references from people you know who have done this type of program.

If you don't know anyone to turn to, let your fingers do the walking down the telephone listings of sound studios in your area. If you are in a large town, one or more studios will specialize in this type of production as opposed to making records or commercials. Find out which ones and do some price comparisons. Keep in mind there will be two costs—one for recording time in the studio and one for editing time. There may be other costs, so be sure to get an all-inclusive price estimate. Studios have either in-house announcers or some type of affiliation with other voices you can rent. Usually, they'll have a demo reel with a few seconds each of several different talents. Pick the one you like and again negotiate the price. If you're in a town that doesn't have a professional studio, call your local radio station. In fact, better than that, pick out the announcer's voice you like the best and call him or her. Tell them what you need done and ask if they do those types of tapes. I think you'll be pleasantly surprised at how many people in radio and television are willing to do this type of work on the side. Most of them can also tell you where to find the proper studio. Some even have arrangements where they work to produce sound tapes. When it comes time to get the audio track taped, you direct the talent if at all possible. Only you know how the finished tape should sound.

Working with a professional studio will give you some more options for your program: namely, music and sound effects. Most studios that specialize in these types of recordings either lease or buy both. Put a little music at the beginning and end and include the appropriate sound effects (if needed), and your program will quickly lose its amateur standing.

If, after you've used all the techniques we discussed here, you're looking for an even smoother program, get a dissolve unit. If you're not familiar with the term, that's a mechanical device that bridges the slides from two projectors onto one screen. As the image from one slide dissolves, a slide from the opposite projector fades onto the screen—thus, absolutely no flashes of light between slides. The next step up is to go into a small programmer. But that topic leads to more complicated programs. Being true to my word of confining this book to basics, I'll stop right here on this topic.

Multiscreen Presentations

So far, we've been dealing with single-screen, single-image presentations. And, as a leader of small conferences, you'll undoubtedly use these techniques the most. I hope I've imparted some new tips and refreshed your memory on others to the depth you need to produce a first-class slide presentation. In the next chapter, I'll acquaint you with the techniques used in producing multiscreen, multimedia, and multi-image presentations.

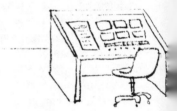

Multiscreen, Multimedia, and Multi-Image Presentations

Computers can figure out all kinds of problems,
except the things in this world that just don't add up.
                                    —JAMES MAGARY

Just Scratching the Surface

Let's get one thing straight from the beginning of this chapter. This is an overview. Its purpose is to give you a nodding acquaintance with the techniques used in producing multiple images on a single or on multiple screens.

We're not trying to be antagonistic about it—we're merely making the point that it is a broad topic. And at the high end of the field, specialized techniques and expensive equipment are needed. However, on the low end, simple two- and three-screen presentations can be put together rather easily. We'll share a few tips with you on how that's done.

In the Beginning, There Are Storyboards

These take a slightly different form than the storyboards we used for our single-screen presentation. Their usage is the same—a picture in each box and script alongside. The blocks are filled in as the audience will view them. (I only bring that up because stage directions are confusing to most people because they are the opposite of the audience's left and right.)

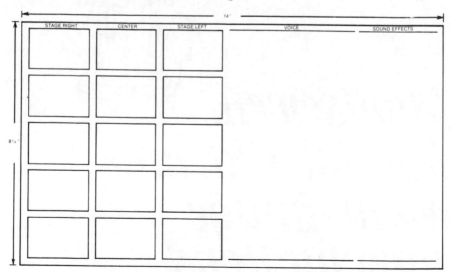

Figure 16-1. (a) Format paper for three-screen presentations.

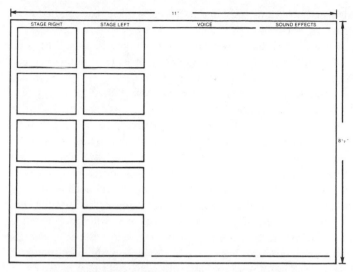

(b) Format paper for two-screen presentations.

Two-Screen Presentations

Two-screen presentations can be extremely effective if they're done well. And most presentations can be adapted to two screens; however, they should be *written* in that format. It's not just a matter of ping-ponging slides from one screen to the other, but rather a matter of continuing a sustaining thread on one screen while more short-range topics are covered on the other.

Here's a "for instance." If we were going to put our story of housing into a two-screen format, I would put "people pictures" on the screen on the auditorium right (stage left) and the housing on the other screen. The ratio of housing slides to people slides would be about 3 to 1. As we showed the caveman, we would run through all of the different types of shelters he could have used. Next, a shot of an Indian or aborigine on the people screen, then all of the different types of housing they occupied on the other, and so on throughout the presentation.

A two-screen presentation I did recently comes to mind. The occasion was the honoring of a famous missionary on her eighty-first birthday. It was quite a story. She had started at age twenty as a fresh college graduate, and stuck with it until she was seventy-five years old. During her career, she had been honored by presidents, congressmen, church dignitaries, and was personally decorated with a medal by the emperor of Japan.

I told this story on two screens. The pictures on the stage-left screen were all of her. They began with her at an early age, then gradually showed her growing older. The pictures on the "action screen" covered the main events of those various periods of her life. The narration was done with a male narrator giving a voice-over presentation. This was interspersed with audio portions made up by three different women's voices, plus appropriate music. The three women portrayed the honoree and two of her close friends. The effect was magnificent, but, as with all visual programs, we have to fall back on saying you had to be there to appreciate it.

There was a funny little aside to this presentation. It doesn't have anything to do with A/V particularly, but it was the basis of a warm and continuing relationship with the central character of the program.

The research, writing, and production were all clothed in secrecy until the program was shown on the appointed evening. The basic information on the lady's life was snitched from an autobiographical journal she kept. This was enriched and elaborated on through conversations with her friends, acquaintances, and church and civil officials. The lady was not aware that any of this was going on.

Concurrently, and unknown to me, the lady was being interviewed for a series of future newspaper articles. When the missionary saw her life unfold, her quick mind led her to conclude that the newspaper reporter had written the program. Given the circumstances, that was not an illogical conclusion to reach.

The upshot came at the coffee and cake reception that followed. She wanted the program writer to stand beside her for a while in the reception line. The MC brought me up and introduced me while the lady was trying to see over or around my 6-foot 3-inch male bulkiness to locate the 105-pound woman she thought had written the program. In her words, "The sweet little girl from the *Houston Chronicle*."

It took a while, but we got it all straightened out and all had a good laugh. Since then, when I call her on the telephone, I always introduce myself as the "sweet little . . ."

The inside joke is like the program. We can write all we want to about it, but you had to be there to really appreciate either. And that's the way of all really good A/V programs. They're not written to be read; they are sounds to hear and visual impressions to see.

Here's another way you could use a similar technique. In huge meeting rooms with audiences numbering in the hundreds, not everyone can see the speaker. With a two-screen arrangement, you can put slides of the speaker on one screen and carry his or her message on the other. We've also seen a similar technique used within presentations, where, in addition to the two regular screens, the speaker's picture appeared on a smaller screen directly above and behind the lectern.

Obviously, moving up from one screen to two takes more care in preparation. Loosely translated, that means more time and money. You'll notice that is a recurring theme as we move up through the balance of this chapter.

Three-Screen Presentations

As promised, three-screen presentations will take more of your time and money. Joking aside—there is enough of both involved to make you think twice about using the technique often. But when the occasion calls for it, they are darned impressive.

When producing or scripting three-screen presentations, all of the storyboard and slide production techniques are consistent with those used for single-screen shows. There are two added tenets, though. Each slide must be simple in form and related to the other two that are visible.

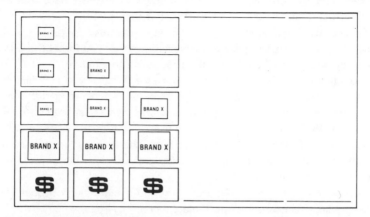

Figure 16-2. A completed page of a three-screen presentation.

The move across the screens left to right and making the product grow becomes interesting (up to a point), but you wouldn't want to use it to introduce each point. But as you vary techniques, be careful to keep every slide change in synchronization with the words and in relation to the other visible slides. One last word of financial caution: *Three screens take a lot of fodder, so even if you are self-producing this type of presentation, be prepared to spend a bundle on slides.*

Multimedia and Multi-Image Shows— Costly but Dazzling!

In addition to the standard three-screen presentation, multiscreen shows are written using a variety of other techniques. One of these is multimedia, in which several different projection methods are used—slides, overheads, and motion pictures, in various permutations and combinations.

Multi-image is the process of adding variety to the kinds of images that the audience sees; various masks are used on the screens or slides to alter image size from the standard 3 x 2 format. This technique permits using a number of projectors on a portion of the screen. By rapidly changing the slides or other projected images, it is possible to obtain many unusual—and often striking—effects. There can be the illusion that pictures are being built or dismantled, or about anything else your imagination can conceive.

If you are interested in producing multimedia or multi-image shows, there are two ways of doing it. The first—and probably most desirable—way is to hire a professional production company, tell them what you want, and work with them. It's costly, time-consuming, and if done well, dazzling. The second way also takes a lot of time, a lot of money, and a lot of dedication. The time is to educate yourself in techniques, available equipment, and equipment capability. The money is to buy or rent a helluva lot of expensive equipment. And the dedication is to go through the long and extremely complex drill of putting together a show that is perfectly synchronized to take advantage of the fast pace and dazzling effects that make multimedia shows worth what they cost.

Unless you are planning to go into the multimedia business professionally and produce these shows on a regular basis, we suggest that you forget the whole idea of producing one yourself and leave the production to experts.

A production company can do some other nice things if you pick one that has the latest in sophisticated equipment. For example, some production companies use a continuous screen that is the same size and format as three (or more) separate screens. With a combination of various slide masks and dissolve units, panoramas can be built that fill the entire screen. There are an endless number of special effects that can be developed by using a greater number of projectors and slide masks in a variety of combinations.

If you have the right production company and a big enough budget, the only limits to special effects are your own imagination.

Recommended Reading

Please don't think that we are "copping out" in this chapter. We have given you the best advice we know how to give. It takes an entire book to begin to tell you what you need to know about this complicated subject. Fortunately, one is available, and we suggest you read it—even if you decide to go to a production company. This way, you'll be able to hold an intelligent conversation and know what everyone is talking about as you write up the contract and make the arrangements.

The book we recommend—and we consider it the "bible" for multimedia production—is:

Images, Images, Images
The Book of Programmed Multi-Image Production
Eastman Kodak Company, 1979 (Price, $15.95)

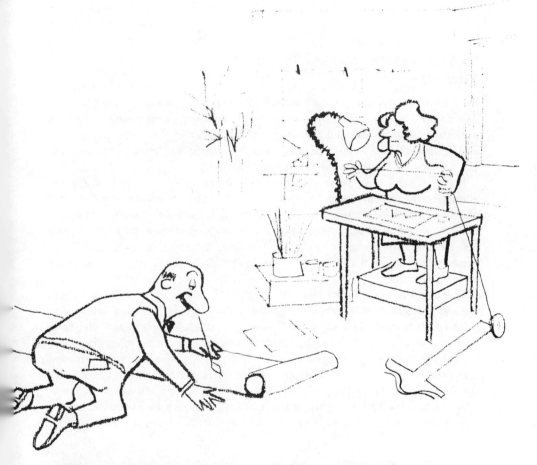

Designing Visuals –
Basics for the
Do-It-Yourselfer

If you want a job done right, do it yourself.

— ANCIENT ADAGE

So You Want to Make the Visuals Yourself

Let's start with the end product: in the beginning, yours probably aren't going to look as good as those done by a professional. That statement wasn't made as a put-down. Quality slides and overhead cells are a matter of training, experience, and equipment. You at this time may be light on all three. That doesn't mean you can't or shouldn't try to make presentable visuals.

Keep in mind that, while this chapter and the following chapters are not intended to replace an education in art or photography, they will give you distinct advantages over most laypersons. You will be taken behind the production scenes to learn enough to direct art and photography work. And these chapters will give you the basic knowledge of how to do visuals at a fraction of the cost of hiring someone else to do them (that is, if you don't initially put too high a cost factor on your own time).

Quick and dirty can sometimes be adequate. For instance, training managers use lots and lots of simple slides and overhead transparencies. They can usually get by with homemade ones. In fact, some of the training managers who have been at it for a while can do as well as most pros. And, there are others fortunate enough to work for companies that have art departments or at least an in-house artist who can do layouts for overhead cells or slides. But for the rest of our readers, we'll offer a few techniques. Not only will these cover quick and dirty, but in later chapters we'll present some of the polished techniques used by professionals.

The sequence in which we'll present this information in this chapter and later chapters is:

- Transparency copying
- Layout and design
- Getting the artwork on paper (or transparency)
- Camera work for slides
- Some additional techniques used in slide preparation

Overhead Cells in Basic Black

Overhead cells in black and white or black with a colored background are no sweat. All you need is some simple artwork and access to a machine that will transfer the artwork to a transparency. There is an entire class of machines manufactured to do just that. Three of the better-known names in the transparency business are A. B. Dick (Master Transparency Maker™), 3M Company (Secretary™) and Ditto (Masterfax™). If you can get to one of these machines with your artwork, you can make an excellent reproduction onto a transparency. That takes about one minute, and these are dry processes, so the transparency is ready to use. *One caution: The artwork must be prepared with a heat-absorbing material such as carbon-based ink or soft lead pencil. If the original material will not transfer, you can make a copy on a regular copy machine and then use that as the master.*

Adding color. There is a range of single-color transparencies available for transferring machines. You can buy either the type of transparency that gives you colored letters on a clear background or the type that gives you clear letters on a colored background. Another option is to use colored felt-tip marking pens or highlighters to add color accents to your black-and-white transparencies.

Slightly downscale from transparencies made on the machines mentioned earlier are those made on a regular copy machine. Most Xerox and many other brands of copy machines will turn out acceptable transparencies. Also, you can make transparencies on Xerox color copiers. If you are not certain whether the copy machine you plan to use will make transparencies, talk to the manufacturer or sales representative for that brand. If it won't do the job, you still have the option of getting copies made at a quick-stop copy business. As easy as the copy machine people have made it for us, the biggest chore is art production. Usually art is prepared separately and transferred as we have described. But you can, if you wish, do the art directly on the transparency. Either way, the principles remain the same.

Layout and Design

"The" rule in designing or laying out an overhead cell is *keep it simple*. Messages need to be short and in letters large enough to be easily read.

The message does not have to be spelled out in its entirety if you are going to elaborate on it orally. And, remember, *if the message can't be seen, don't show it!*

Here is a short portion of an article that appeared in a local newspaper (*Houston Post,* September 30, 1979, Section B, p. 2):

> The movement of Americans from the rural areas into the cities, which has been going on since the beginning of the century, has reversed itself. People are now moving out of the cities at a faster rate than those moving in from the country are replacing them, and all the signs suggest that they will continue to do so . . .

For the sake of illustration, let's say that you were making a presentation on consumer demographics and wanted to visualize this scrap of information as part of your message. The first rule, of course, is to research the article to authenticate the information and get hard statistics to back it up. With the facts in hand, you can visualize this bit of information in a number of ways—always, however, taking care to ensure legibility, clarity of layout, and consistency with the remainder of your visuals. These principles of design apply either to overhead transparencies or slides. Most of the artwork shown on the following pages can also be used as the basis for slides. Keep in mind, though, that the formats are slightly different.

Various types of artwork for design. Let's look at some various types of artwork for design. Then, in the next section, we'll prepare the art for each cell. The layouts began by making draft sheets to correct format. For overhead cells, that's 9½ x 7½ inches. The simplest way to stay in format is to make a template or buy a blank overhead cell mount. Draw a faint border by using the inside edge of the mask as a guide. Then lay out the artwork within the border.

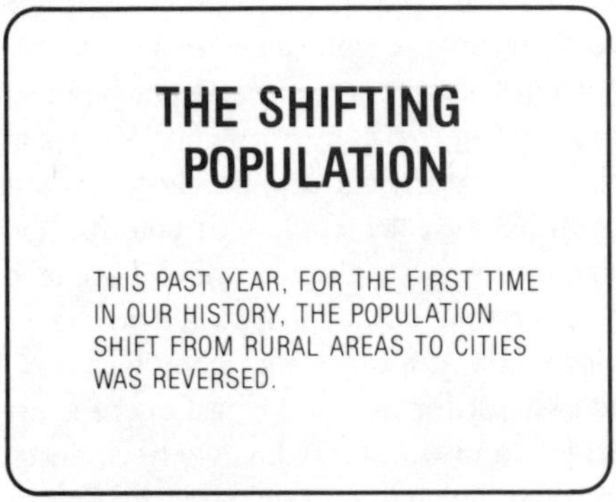

THE SHIFTING POPULATION

THIS PAST YEAR, FOR THE FIRST TIME IN OUR HISTORY, THE POPULATION SHIFT FROM RURAL AREAS TO CITIES WAS REVERSED.

Figure 17-1. *Straight copy.* **This should be centered with wide margins and lots of open space. Headlines should be 36 points or larger (½ inch) and body copy should be 18 points or larger. More words would make this design cluttered and hard to read. The speaker can further elaborate on the point being made here.**

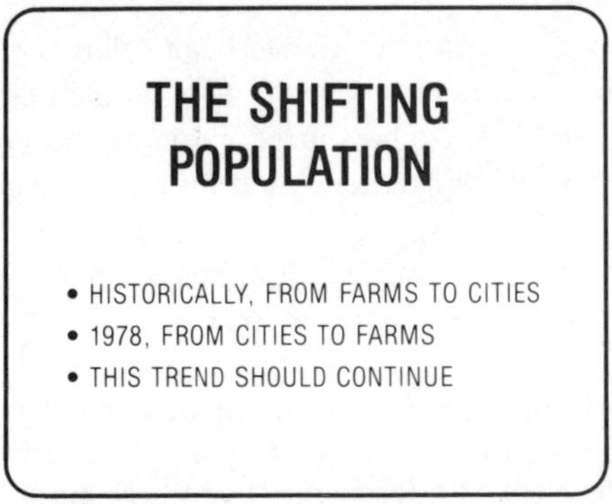

THE SHIFTING POPULATION

- HISTORICALLY, FROM FARMS TO CITIES
- 1978, FROM CITIES TO FARMS
- THIS TREND SHOULD CONTINUE

Figure 17-2. *Bullet outline.* **This type of outline does three things. (1) It contains more of the message for the audience; (2) it helps the speaker by doubling as a cue card; and (3) the lesser number of words allows for both spacing and balance. This copy could also be used as a reveal-type cell.**

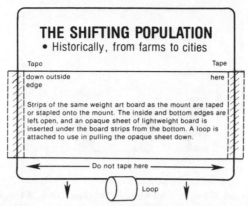

Figure 17-3. *The reveal.* Sometimes called the dramatic reveal, this is merely a single overhead cell that has a sliding opaque screen affixed. As the speaker finishes speaking about one line of copy, the loop is used to pull the screen down far enough to reveal the next line and so on until each line is revealed in sequence.

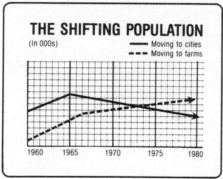

Figure 17-4. *The graph.* In the graph format, hard statistical information can be charted. With it you visually transmit exact data and show long-range trends.

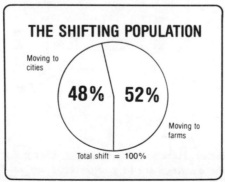

Figure 17-5. *The pie chart.* This technique works best when used to show a single set of statistics on a percentage basis. It could be used here provided it was adequately supported by the speaker's narrative.

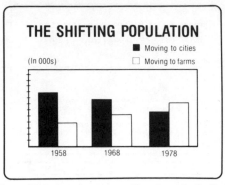

Figure 17-6. *Bar chart.* **This can be very effective. And, if the speaker wanted to dramatize this point, the chart could be made to grow by using a series of overlays.**

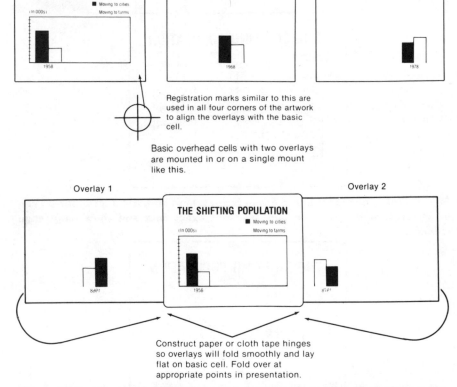

Registration marks similar to this are used in all four corners of the artwork to align the overlays with the basic cell.

Basic overhead cells with two overlays are mounted in or on a single mount like this.

Construct paper or cloth tape hinges so overlays will fold smoothly and lay flat on basic cell. Fold over at appropriate points in presentation.

Figure 17-7. *The overlay.* **Here's how to put together a bar chart that grows. The basic cell and the overlays are in a registered series. The basic cell contains the background chart and the first set of statistics. The two overlays show one statistic per chart. The same technique can be used on a horizontal bar chart or to make one continuous line grow in length by adding to the bars with each overlay.**

Figure 17-8. *Symbolism.* Let's depart a bit further from words to some simple ways of putting the same message in symbols. The corresponding large picture is the one on which this passage will end. It's part of an overlay. There is another overlay prior to that on the same cell, but on it the arrows point toward the city instead of away from it.

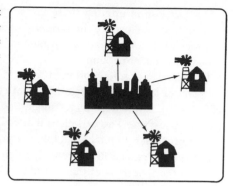

OVERLAY 1   OVERLAY 2

Figure 17-9. Here's how we got there. We began with a basic cell of farms and a city and two overlays, one with arrows pointing toward the city, one with arrows pointing away from the city. We started the sequence with overlay 1 folded flat on top of the basic cell and overlay 2 open. When the speaker finished talking about the historic movement to cities, overlay 1 was put in the open poisiton and overlay 2 was placed over the basic cell, thus reversing the arrows. This visually reversed the population shift for the audience.

Figure 17-10. *The single symbol.* This type of symbolism is fine if you're the kind of speaker who can carry it off. It requires a bit looser approach but it still conveys the basic idea—and at a glance.

Figure 17-11. *Picture only.* Envision this approach. "More people are saying thumbs up to living in the country. This past year more of them made that move . . ."

Our purpose in offering these various ways of presenting a short message is twofold: first, to illustrate the proper amount of copy and how to balance it on the cell; second, to show there are a number of ways to visualize the same message through the same medium.

This offering of a few different ways to say the same thing is by no means all-inclusive. In fact, it's just a start to what can be done—I know I could have gone on for two or three more pages suggesting additional visuals on the same topic—and that's just me. The variations that could come with different experiences and mental processes infinitely multiply the possibilities.

If that's the case, you're probably asking, then, which one is right? The answer is any of them or none of them. What makes a visual *right* depends on a number of things—but the basic tests are:

- Is the design good?
- Is the meaning simple to grasp?
- Does it convey the true thought?
- Is it compatible with other visuals in the same presentation?
- Does it fit the words in style and tone that the speaker will employ? (Highly formal charts may not fit the loose, oral approach of some speakers—or vice versa.)

Pick the approach that you think is best for you. Storyboard a few visuals and try them out—along with the words—on an unbiased listener who will give you constructive feedback. Whatever your approach, keep in mind the tests each visual should pass: legibility, clarity, and compatibility.

Artwork for Transparencies and Slides – Letters and Numbers

How can you contrive to write so even?

— JANE AUSTEN

The Answer to Jane Austen's Question

As we have just shown, there are a variety of ways to visualize the same message. There are also several ways to produce the art for each type of visual mechanically. We'll share as many of these techniques as space permits within the printing budget. Almost all of our examples have either some words or some numbers (or both) incorporated, so we'll start with them.

Lettering Techniques

The first and most obvious way of lettering is by hand. That can be done on paper and then transferred by machine onto the cell, or you can write directly on the cell with special pens. The pens mentioned in an earlier chapter will work or you can simply ask your local art dealer what else is available.

For more formal lettering, there are other methods you can use. Let's see if we can broaden your horizons by offering an even ten ways to get words on paper or directly on a transparency. *One word of caution: although the process is the same, whether putting letters on paper or a transparency, the materials are different.* When you are putting your message on paper, you'll want to use opaque materials and inks, and in most cases those containing a high degree of carbon. Working directly on a transparency, you need translucent materials that don't totally block off the light of the projector.

All of the methods offered here (short of buying a lettering machine) can give you reasonable artwork with a minimum initial *financial* investment. We stress financial investment because, until you become accustomed to working with these, you'll have some time invested in preparing transparencies with them.

Dry-transfer letters. The method most professionals use day in and day out is dry-transfer letters. You can buy these at almost all art supply stores and at many office supply stores. In fact, the art store we generally use has an entire department devoted to various forms of dry-transfer type, and a variety of backgrounds and symbols on gummed film. On the counter are huge catalogues showing the various typefaces and sizes of letters and numbers, along with the variety of matching materials that are available for purchase. There are literally thousands of both.

Let's get one thing straight in our vocabulary—that's point size of type. Being mere mortals and Americans at that, we're used to measuring things in inches, feet, yards, and so on. Printers, typesetters, and sellers of dry-transfer letters don't. They measure in point size. *Don't despair. There is a translation:*

12 points = 1 pica, and 6 picas = 1 inch

In lay terms, a letter that is ½ inch tall (according to us) is 36 points in their jargon. Thus, 24-point letters are ⅔ of an inch, 18-point letters are ¼ of an inch, and 12 points are ⅙ of an inch—and that's as small as I'm going to go. And that is as small as you'll ever want to go in laying out artwork. In fact, you're better off staying with 18-point or larger letters.

Dry-transfer letters are sold by the sheet. Sheets from the same manufacturer are the same size, so the number of letters you get depends on the point size. (Smaller letters = more on a page.)

Dry-transfer letters are affixed with a waxy substance to the bottom or downside of a transparent sheet of thin plastic. They are protected on the back by a second sheet of wax paper. With the protective sheet lifted out of the way, the letters are lined up over the artwork, then the top sheet is rubbed with a stylus immediately over the letter to be transferred. The rubbing action sets the letter to the artwork original. The artwork can be paper or it can be the transparency itself. But once again, if you are going directly to the transparency, use translucent letters.

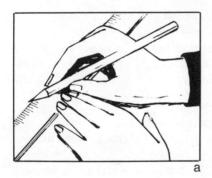
a

b

c

Figure 18-1. Three steps for dry-transfer letters: (*a*) Set up your guide lines. (*b*) Remove the protective backing and position the type over the guide lines. Then transfer each letter individually by rubbing the top sheet with a stylus. (*c*) Using a clear film as a protective sheet and the broad end of the stylus, iron the letters down.

Aligning the letters on the artwork can be done in a number of ways. The most common are to draw faint pencil lines, use them for guides, and then erase them; or to inscribe faint blue lines that won't reproduce on a copy machine; or to insert a piece of ruled or graph paper under the artwork and light it from below so the shadows cast give you temporary guidelines.

Most professionals use the third technique, since with them a light table is standard equipment. You can create the same effect by propping up a piece of plastic or plate glass and lighting it from the bottom with an ordinary light bulb. I have personally built a couple of deluxe light tables, but in earlier days, I used a square of plate glass and a 25-watt bulb. Currently, I have an inexpensive drawing board in my home that has a center insert of milk-white plastic. It cost me $17 to build and I use it for a number of things—tracing, which we'll talk more about later, setting press-on type, and—with a 150-watt bulb in place—I use it as a sorting surface for slides. (Incidentally, we'll talk more about that later, too.)

While we're on the subject of light tables, here's a clever idea that Jeff had. Like many trainers and seminar leaders, Jeff has a portable overhead projector that he takes along with him when his client doesn't have one. The rest of the time, he keeps it set up on a table in his office, with a 12 x 12 inch square of window glass on top of the projection Fresnel lens. That way he can use it as a light table and cut to his heart's content without damaging the Fresnel. It works great, and the only extra expense was the little pane of glass that he picked up at the neighborhood lumberyard.

If you use translucent dry-transfer letters applied directly to a transparency, you'll need to clean off the bits of residual wax you'll transfer along with the letters. Also, don't expect a directly transferred cell to hold up as long as one that is made as a copy. With age and flexing of the transparency, the letters can crack or fall off. But if it is a transparency you expect to use only a few times, they'll hold up for that.

Gum-backed letters. Formatt® is the name of one of the brands of gum-backed letters we use. This company also has a wide range of available symbols, arrows, stars, background designs, and so on. This type of letter cannot go directly on the transparency. You have to put it on paper, then copy. Some of their background material can be pasted directly on transparencies.

Formatt® type is set on a very thin film with a gummed back. It's loosely pasted down on a second sheet. Using an art knife, cut out the letters you want to use without cutting through the back sheet, pull the letters you want from the second sheet, and press them into place on your artwork. The use of some of their symbols along with the lettering can add up to a good-looking piece of art.

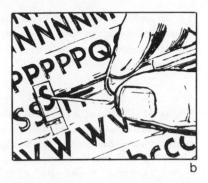

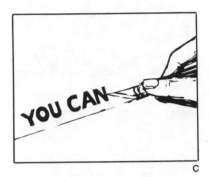

a

b

c

Figure 18-2. Three steps for using gum-backed type: (a) Set up your guide lines on the back of your artwork so they show through. Do not put guide marks on the face side of your paper. (b) Cut the *film only* that holds the desired letter onto the backing sheet. Lift the letter off with the point of an art knife. (c) Using the flat of the blade of an art knife, slide each letter into place; press it down tight to the paper.

Commercially set type. In every large city there is at least one typesetting house. These people are in the business of setting type for reproduction. The bigger ones may not want to fool around with the small amount of type required for a handful of overhead cells, but the smaller houses usually are willing.

Type houses have a chart or catalog with all of their available typefaces and point sizes. Pick out what you want, write out the message, and they can furnish it to you in a number of different ways: on plain paper, on wax-backed paper that you can stick down, or in strips.

Some houses can furnish you with the type already set on transparencies, or already glued up in perfect format so all you have to do is make a copy onto the transparency. As usual, a word of caution: *check the price before you commit yourself, and use the type as soon as possible after you receive it.* Some of the type set this way has a tendency to fade with time.

If you decide to go this route, check your spelling and grammar carefully before you send your copy to the type house. You're probably going to get back exactly what you sent, complete with misspelled words. Also, when you receive the type, check their spelling and spacing. If they've made a mistake, they'll correct it at no charge. If the mistake is yours, you'll have to pay for corrections.

Diecut letters. This is another item carried by art supply stores and many stationers. These are made from paper or vinyl mounted on a second sheet. Peel 'em off and slap 'em down. Well, almost. Some brands have little fingers that hold these in place on the mounting sheets. These may leave an irregular edge on one or more places around the letter. Scrape these edges clear with an art knife, then slap 'em down.

Figure 18-3. Diecut letters: (a) Press-out letters often have minorly jagged edges where they joined the backing sheet. (b) When the letter is projected several times its original dimensions, the jags become more obvious. (c) If these are pronounced, scrape them off the letters with an art knife before you glue the letters in place.

a

b

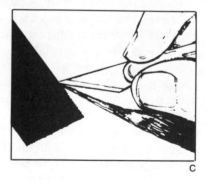

c

So far, that's five ways you can get the lettering down on your artwork—by hand, dry transfer, gum-backed, set type, and diecut. Some of the remaining ways require equipment. I'll plunge ahead in the hope that you have access to one or more of these types of equipment—but didn't know you could use it for these purposes.

Lettering templates. The cheapest equipment-assisted method of hand lettering is with manual lettering templates. If you were born in the age of plastic, as a kid, you probably had a ruler with a lettering guide cut into it. (Those little cutouts you used to letter your boyfriend's or girlfriend's name in your notebook while you were supposed to be doing your homework.) Commercial letter guides are merely an upgraded version of these. They cost more, they're more exact, but they oper-

ate on the same principle. You lay the guide on the artwork and, with a pen or pencil, trace around the inside edges of the cutout. You can buy an individual commercial template for $2 or $3.

Figure 18-4. Lettering templates: (*a*) With a fine-tip pen or pencil (you can buy one made especially for this job), make an outline of each letter desired. (*b*) Then, if you wish, broaden each letter with a wider felt-tip marker.

Pantograph. A pantograph and a template set allow you to do the same thing, but, with the proper setting, you can enlarge or reduce the size of the letters.

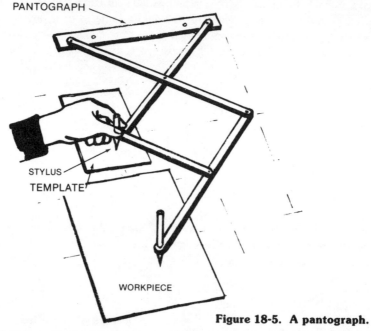

Figure 18-5. A pantograph.

Lettering Machines. Verigraph, Leroy, and other lettering machines are found in some offices, especially those of engineering firms. Although I've used them for artwork, I wouldn't buy one to use only for overhead transparencies—unless, of course, I was going to make a lot of them. I've seen some models of lettering machines priced on the low end of the scale at about $100. There is another way, though, of looking at this type of purchase. If you are paying $40 to $50 per transparency, it doesn't take you long to get your money back from a lettering machine.

When using a template or lettering machine and you want letters that are fatter than one pen stroke, do what the pros do. Draw thin outlines around the edges of the letters. Then fill the outlines in with a broad-stroke, felt-tip pen.

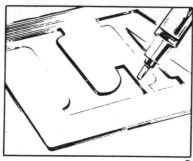

a   b

Figure 18-6. Creating wide letters: (a) Draw around the outline, and (b) **fill the outlined letters with a broad felt-tip pen.**

Self-operated typeset machines. The Visual Product Division of 3M Company sells a lettering system that consists of a machine, lettering tapes, and a variety of discs of different typefaces. The disc can be mounted and dismounted easily by the operator. The disc with the correct typeface is mounted on the machine. The operator rotates the disc by hand as the words are spelled out, letter by letter, onto gum-backed, lightweight film. The film is stuck down on the artwork and then put through the copying process to get it on the transparency. This machine is often sold as a companion to the 3M Secretary™ copier. The tapes it produces have the correct density and amount of carbon for good reproduction on the Secretary™.

The tenth way. So far, I covered nine ways to get lettering on artwork and I promised ten, so here's the last one. Buy an alphabet book and trace the letters onto your artwork.

Art stores sell books for that purpose. You'll want to make sure that the book you buy is intended for reproduction in part by the consumer.

Usually, you use lightweight white paper over the characters in the book and trace lightly around each letter. Then the book is removed and the lettering on the artwork is filled in with heavier pen strokes. This work can be aided by working on a light table and lighting the artwork from below. That should make it easier when you're tracing anything. This entire operation can be a little slow, but your initial investment is low, and your master alphabets are reusable indefinitely.

As promised, you now have ten possible ways to get letters and numbers on artwork. Don't take these as all-inclusive. There are other ways that will spring from your creative imagination as you get into producing your own visuals. With the lettering done, you have won half the battle. The next step is to combine the letters with symbols, background, and pictures into finished artwork.

Artwork for Transparencies and Slides – Adding Graphs, Symbols, and Pictures

The artist drew a great many lines and saved the best of them.

— SAMUEL BUTLER

Anything's Easy If You Know How

The list of inside tips that are set forth in this chapter is not to be construed as complete. That would take another book as long as this one is already. Rather than try to tell you every conceivable way of preparing artwork, we'll zero in on a few materials and techniques, primarily the ones used in preparing the artwork shown in Chapter 17.

Materials

There are three broad categories for these types of materials: dry transfer, pressure sensitive (gum-backed film), and clip art. Dry transfer and some types of pressure-sensitive materials can be applied directly to transparencies, provided the applied materials transmit light. Or any of these materials can be applied to paper artwork and, through the copy process, transferred to transparencies.

It would be impossible to list every manufacturer of these materials—I simply don't know all of the brand names, but let me pass along to you some of the names I do know:

Dry-transfer brands	*Pressure-sensitive brands*
Prestype™	Miro™ type
ChartPak®	Formatt®
Instantype™	Formaline®
Tacttype™	

Clip-art suppliers (write for their catalogues)

Dynamic Graphics, Inc.	Pictorial Archive Dept.
6707 North Sheridan Road	Dover Publications, Inc.
P. O. Box 1901	180 Varick Street
Peoria, IL 61656	New York, NY 10014

Or check your local art store's book rack for other clip-art books.

Some materials from each category—plus drawing pens and construction paper—were used to produce the art in our earlier examples (the population shift from city to rural life). Let's go back through the examples from Chapter 17 and discuss how each was completed.

Combining Materials and Techniques

Figures 19-1, 19-2, and 19-3 are all straight copy, so they could have been prepared using any one of the ten lettering processes detailed earlier. All of them produce basic lettering; some permit you to put the words in color directly on the transparency. (However, and just as a point of information, all of these were prepared with dry-transfer type on paper artwork and transferred to the transparency.)

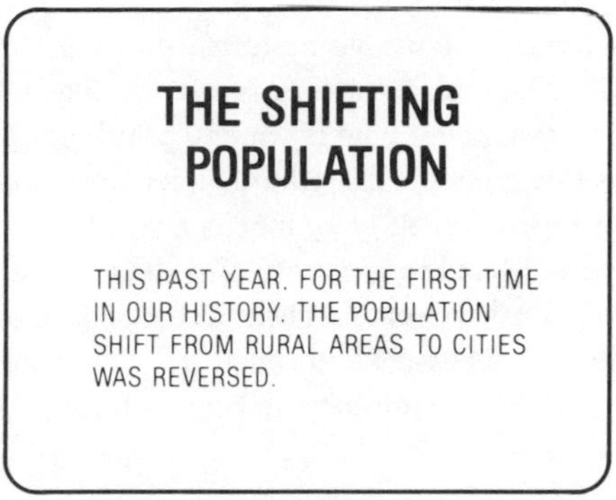

THE SHIFTING
POPULATION
THIS PAST YEAR, FOR THE FIRST TIME
IN OUR HISTORY, THE POPULATION
SHIFT FROM RURAL AREAS TO CITIES
WAS REVERSED.

Figure 19-1. A straight-copy transparency prepared with dry-transfer type.

THE SHIFTING
POPULATION
• HISTORICALLY, FROM FARMS TO CITIES
• 1978, FROM CITIES TO FARMS
• THIS TREND SHOULD CONTINUE

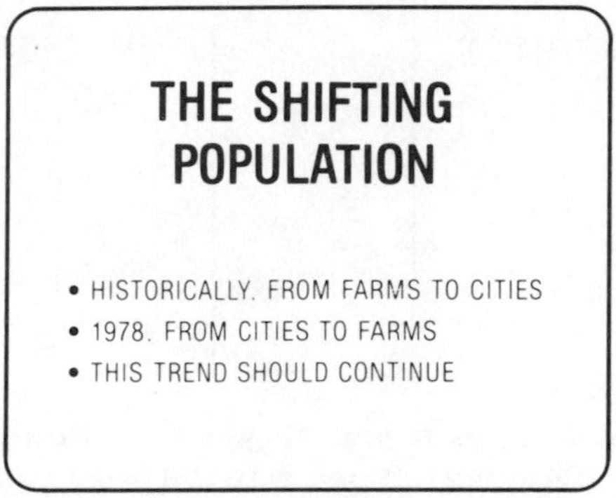

Fgiure 19-2. Any of the ten lettering processes described in Chapter 17 could have been used to prepare these straight-copy transparencies.

THE SHIFTING POPULATION
• Historically, from farms to cities
Tape
Tape
down outside
edge
here
Strips of the same weight art board as the mount are taped or stapled onto the mount. The inside and bottom edges are left open, and an opaque sheet of lightweight board is inserted under the board strips from the bottom. A loop is attached to use in pulling the opaque sheet down.
Do not tape here
Loop

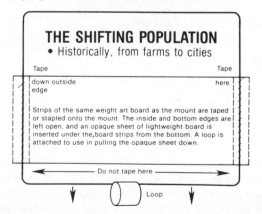

Figure 19-3. Color can be added to straight-copy transparencies to make them more interesting.

Beginning with Figure 19-4, additional materials are needed.

Graphs and lines. *Figures 19-4 through 19-7.* We've almost beaten to death the discussion about lettering, so let's deal only with the new elements—the graph and lines.

The graph itself is pressure-sensitive material, and the trend lines are narrow pressure-sensitive tape. The graph material is a stock item—but if you were preparing the art on paper, you could glue down any graph paper of the appropriate size; that is, provided the rules on the graph paper are black. The regular blue ruled material doesn't reproduce in copy machines.

Pressure-sensitive tape is sold in a variety of widths, a spectrum of colors, and a range of styles—dots, dashes, solid, translucent, opaque, and so on.

All of the artwork in Figures 19-4 through 19-7 was actually produced on paper, then transferred to a transparency. In correct format, it could just as easily be photographed for a slide.

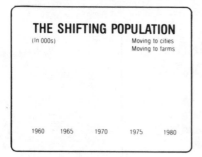

Figure 19-4. The basic chart is prepared with pressure-sensitive letters and numbers.

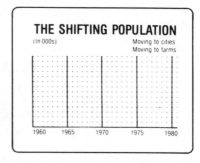

Figure 19-5. Pressure-sensitive graph material is pressed on.

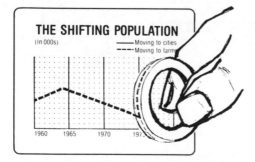

Figure 19-6. Trend lines are made with narrow pressure-sensitive tape (several designs on this are available—dotted line, broken line, and solid line, in a variety of widths).

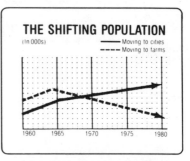

Figure 19-7. Two different styles of pressure-sensitive tape are used. The finished artwork is then transferred to a transparency.

Figures 19-8 and 19-9. The new element here is the pie chart. The type for this transparency was set on paper, then transferred to the cell, and the pie chart was added, using two contrasting colors of pressure-sensitive overlay material.

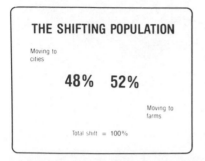

Figure 19-8. The basic chart is pre-pared using dry-transfer or pressure-sensitive letters and numbers, then transferred to a transparency.

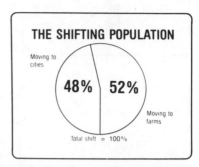

Figure 19-9. Two colors of pressure sensitive, translucent overlay material can be used to construct the pie. The transparency is then ready for use.

An alternate method would be to prepare the entire piece of art on paper, and use two different densities of background materials to form the pie.

Another alternative would be to construct the pie from colored art paper and make a copy of the chart on a color reproducing copy machine. The resulting transparency would not be quite as crisp as this one, but it would give you the opportunity to use materials you may already have on hand.

Figure 19-10. These examples were prepared using all pressure-sensitive materials. The only new element is the bars. They were constructed by using two different types of background material cut to size and overlayed on the artwork.

To prepare a single transparency, as in Figure 17-6, use one piece of art. To construct the overlayed chart shown here and in Figure 17-7, use three pieces of artwork.

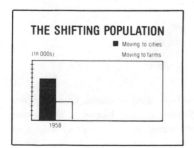

Basic cell

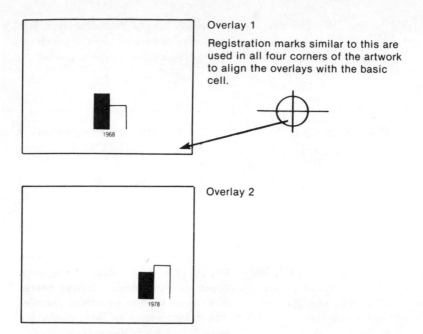

Overlay 1

Registration marks similar to this are used in all four corners of the artwork to align the overlays with the basic cell.

1968

Overlay 2

1978

Figure 19-10. The components are prepared, transferred to three transparencies, and assembled. Overlays are turned as needed during the presentation. The entire cell with both overlays in place would project as a single chart.

Symbols and pictures. Figure 19-11a,b,c. This example begins to veer away from the style set in the earlier examples. It varies in another way—the way the art was prepared. This layout was prepared using clip art and a reducing copy machine.

a

Figure 19-11. (a) The basic cell was prepared by gluing down five clip art barns from Dover's *Handbook of Pictorial Symbols*. The barns, a bit larger than what was needed, were glued in correct format on an oversize sheet of paper.

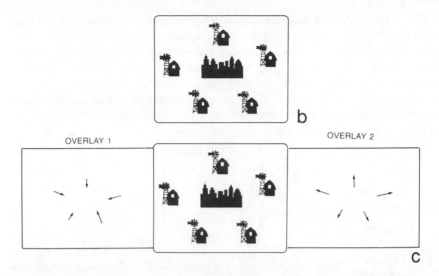

Figure 19-11. (Continued) (*b*) The entire sheet was reduced by 50 percent, then the city was glued on. (*c*) Then the entire piece of art was copied onto the transparency. That completed the basic cell. Paper stock for overlay 1 was layed over the basic cell and clip art arrows were glued in the appropriate places. Then that art was transferred to a transparency. The process, but with the arrows reversed, was repeated for overlay 2.

You may mentally be one step ahead of me and figured that you could have made the arrows with transparent tapes or pressure-sensitive arrows. If you did, you're right. It could be done that way and, if you wish, directly on the overlay transparencies.

Figures 19-12 and 19-13. Two previous elements are combined—dry-transfer letters and two clip-art arrows. (The outlined arrow is laid over one of solid color.)

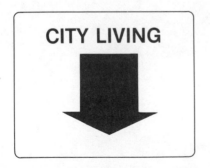

Figure 19-12. Dry-transfer letters and one clip art arrow.

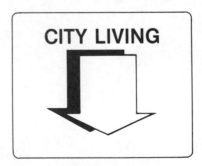

Figure 19-13. Dry-transfer letters and two clip art arrows.

And, again, being a step or two ahead of me, you already may have thought of four or five other ways to get that arrow on the transparency.

Figure 19-14. A new departure. This entire transparency was prepared with water-based, felt-tip pens applied directly. The artwork is the finished product— and it's in color. Here's another tip: *Spray the transparency with a fixative to protect the ink.* If you use this method, here's one more tip that can save you a little time and money: *Prepare your rough sketches in outline form on plain paper, in the correct size and format. Pick the sketch you like best, lay the transparency over it, and trace your outline with a fine-tip pen in the appropriate color. Then fill the large areas with a broad-tip pen of the same shade.*

Figure 19-14. This transparency was prepared with water-based, felt-tip pens applied directly to the transparency.

Professional Tips on Making Slides

Lights . . . Camera . . . Action!

The principles of designing slides are the same as those just offered for overhead cells. Clarity of message, legibility, and compatibility with other slides in the set and the speaker's style are all needed in producing the artwork. All of the materials discussed and most of the techniques for using them are the same in slide production.

Two big differences are the format and the fact that a camera can visualize actual objects instead of drawings or pictures of objects. In this chapter we're going to flip-flop the format. We'll start with the equipment and then give you a few additional techniques for preparing artwork or objects to be photographed.

How Good Is Your Camera?

A brownie box camera won't make it in slide production, but you can get something that will do the job for a modest amount of money. That is, as camera prices go. Although some other cameras will make slides, a 35mm is what you need— if possible, a single-lens reflex.

How good is good enough in a camera is a relative question. Let's see if I can draw an example for you. At this time, I own two camera bodies, which can be used with interchangeable lenses, and one complete camera with a fixed lens. The respective costs were $300, $350, and $129.95. All of them are 35mm, and with the $300 and $350 bodies, lenses have to be purchased extra at $110 and up (and up!). The $129.95 camera takes acceptable photos—in fact, I've taken some shots with it that I consider outstanding. So why did I spend several hundred extra dollars for the more expensive camera bodies? The answer is better control and consistent quality. Both of those are important when making production slides.

Although I often use my $129.95 camera, I never use it for copying artwork into slides. The main usage for that camera is for reference shots of locations and the like. The features that make this camera pay its way are its size (I can put it in my pocket and with the right film I can take pretty fair pictures in low-light situations) and, considering the use I've put it to, it's seemingly indestructible.

The other cameras are a different matter. I use these for heavy production work, sometimes shooting several hundred slides in a week. I know those cameras intimately and know just about what I'm going to get before I trip the shutter.

Does all of this mean you can't take production slides with a $129.95 camera with a fixed lens? No. But you'll have more culls, a wider variance in exposures, and a general loss of crispness in the finished product. There isn't much you can do about it, either. It has to do with the way the camera works and the quality of the lens.

If you understand interworkings of cameras, you'll be able to make knowledgeable corrections in your shooting techniques. I don't want to leave anyone out of this discussion, so let's start at the basic level. The purpose of a camera is to permit *controlled* exposure of photosensitive materials (such as film) to light. The key, and what adds the cost to cameras, is the degree of control. You can make a camera for slow film from a used Quaker Oats box and a very simple lens. You just punch a hole in the side of the box, cover the hole thus punched with a fixed lens and a movable shield or flap, and then tape over all other light-emitting cracks or seams. That's a basic camera. Kids make them in third grade science classes and they work, but in a very limited range and with little control. Building in the controls is where the bucks get spent. And how the controls are built in is what makes the difference in quality.

Controlling the amount of light that enters the camera is done in two ways— the size of the hole in the aperture and the speed at which the shutter opens and closes. In the simplest of cameras, both of these are fixed. Every picture is taken with the same aperture opening or at the same speed. When you move up a notch in quality, one of these factors can be changed by the operator. Or, further up the ladder, you can change both or get an automatic camera that will change both of these settings for you based on the amount of available light (as the camera reads it) and where you have set the film-speed indicator. Moving up a notch in automatic cameras, you can buy one that will allow you to change one of these settings while the camera is in the automatic mode, or you can override this automatic feature and make both of these settings yourself. Somewhere along the way in this progression, you go to what is known as a SLR, or single-lens reflex. What that means is that you are actually focusing through the camera lens instead of a viewfinder. That's important. That feature lets you see the intended exposure as the camera sees it and, with a flick of a button, you can also check the depth of field. That's also important. But let's leave depth of field for later and go back to the two ways you admit light into a camera: aperture opening and speed. Either way lets in the light, and there is a correlation between the two, but there can be a resulting difference in how the finished product looks. The difference depends on which variable you change.

Aperture openings are measured in *f*-stops in what *appears* to be an inverted scale—why this appears to be inverted is because the lower the *f*-stop, the wider the aperture opening. Typically, that scale looks like this:

*f*1.8	*f*2	*f*2.8	*f*4	*f*5.6	*f*8	*f*11	*f*16	*f*22

Speeds run like this:

1000	500	250	125	60	30	15	8	4	2	1

(Fractions of seconds 1000 = $\frac{1}{1000}$ second)

In an automatic camera, when you turn the speed to a higher number, the camera adjusts the *f*-stop to a lower number. (Some automatics work the other way around. The operator sets the *f*-stop and the camera adjusts the speed to a compensating setting. The latter type is called a shutter-priority system. The former is a speed-priority system.) And, although the light is let in for a shorter period of time, the aperture is wider so the film still gets exposed. If you're not a camera buff, your reaction is probably "So what?" Well, here's the "biggie"—and where a lot of pictures get messed up. When you change the *f*-stop, you are also changing the depth of field. Depth of field is what makes your backgrounds clear and crisp or, on the other hand, hazy and out of focus. So what we're really talking about is that in low *f*-stop settings, the focus is much more critical. Thus, more of the photo—foreground and background—is out of focus. In some cases, that's precisely what you want. For instance, you may wish a portrait-type slide with high color saturation and softly mottled background. In forms of advertising photography, some facial features are intentionally thrown slightly out of focus. On the other hand, if you need everything in focus to infinity, shoot at the tight end of the *f* range.

Figure 20-1. Close shot with open *f*-stop (background out of focus).

Figure 20-2. Medium shot with tight *f*-stop (background in sharp focus).

On even the most complicated appearing cameras, there are only four influencing factors: the aperture setting, the shutter speed, the focus, and the film-speed indicator. Matching the film-speed indicator to the ASA number of the film reduces the list to three. Leaving the camera in the automatic mode handles two more of the factors, speed and aperture opening. Thus, your only worry is correct focus. Most shots can be made this way. There are times, though, when you will need to override the automatic settings for special purposes: arresting motion, increasing depth of field to add detail to backgrounds, or purposely throwing backgrounds out of focus. This chart will help you determine how to do this:

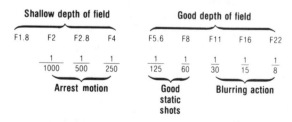

Figure 20-3. A guide to determine shutter speed and *f*-stop.

These figures are correct for cameras equipped with a 55mm or shorter lens. Lenses with longer focal lengths may require a tripod up to speeds of 125 or 250. (The longer the lens, the greater the need for additional support.)

Two points to remember: One, when overriding the automatic controls, you must change both settings, speed and aperture. And, two, with the camera in an automatic mode, when you change one setting, the camera will change the other to compensate. Thus, using the chart above as a reference of relative values, if your camera is metering $f4$ at $\frac{1}{250}$ seconds and you changed the speed to $\frac{1}{500}$, the aperture would open up to $f2.8$ (on a speed-priority camera). On a shutter-priority camera, if you opened the aperture to $f2.8$, the speed would automatically increase to $\frac{1}{500}$.

Many, if not all, of the slides used in A/V programs are shot on a camera stand. Because that one piece of equipment is so important a part of producing good production slides, I have devoted an entire chapter to that one topic. It follows this discussion of the mechanics of cameras.

The most important thing to remember about f-stops is that you stay within the f range. There are four ways that you can do that:

- Altering the shutter speed
- Using sunlight
- Using auxiliary lighting
- Using slower or faster film

Shutter Speed

Usually, the faster the better. Unfortunately, we don't always have that option. So let's talk about the other end of the scale. In hand-held operation, $\frac{1}{60}$ of a second is about the longest an amateur can hold a camera steady with a normal lens. For longer lenses, a good rule of thumb is that minimum shutter speed equals the millimeter (mm) of the lens used. I know pros who can hold a camera steady longer, but even they will use some type of device for steadying the camera at slow shutter speeds. A steadying device can be a number of things, the obvious one being a tripod. But, I've propped cameras on the roofs of cars, table tops, banisters, backs of chairs, and the like. One thing you have to be careful about if you do this is that you don't pick up part of a flat surface as a dark band across the bottom of your photo.

At one time I read about a marvelously simple way of bracing a camera that I want to share with you. I'm sorry that my memory fails me and I can't tell you where I read this. I'd like to because I like to give credit for a good idea where it is due. The device is a short length of sash cord with a small flat piece of metal or wood on one end and a short bolt of the proper thread on the other. The idea is to screw the bolt into the tripod hole in the bottom of your camera and stand on the piece of wood. You then pull up on the camera until the tension of the rope steadies your hands. It won't replace a tripod, but it works.

Any and all of these ideas for steadying a camera are good for general pictorial slides, but for slides made from artwork, you need a copystand of some type. The reason I say "of some type" is that, as you'll see later, that can cover a wide range of equipment.

Natural Light

When you can get it, this is the way to go. The chief advantages are good, even distribution of light—and it's free—nothing to buy, nothing to maintain. Also, with a little effort, you can control the amount of light and shadows you get.

Sometimes, if the weather is right and I have a long run of slides to do, I'll set the copystand up outside and do the shooting there. My favorite place to set up this operation is alongside a building under a wide overhang. The reason for working under the overhang is that it affords a lot of light but it is in consistent shadow. If the day is overcast, I sometimes work out in the direct light, the idea being that natural overcast or an artificial one such as the overhang on the studio reduces the sun's glare and gives almost shadowless lighting. Let's face it—it's also a lot cooler than working in a closed room with two or more 500-watt lamps inches from your face.

There are some ways to control natural sunlight. To reduce glare and shadows, work under an overcast sky or create your own overcast. The overhanging roof idea is one way. You can also construct a simple canopy of thin muslin or nylon net, or you can make a simple sunscreen of cardboard. In working outside, you should keep in mind that a colored sunscreen can cast a reflected tint on your work. Thus, sunscreens or adjacent walls should be neutral in color.

All of these ideas work fine with flat artwork or smooth items. If you are shooting facial shots under a screen or overcast, you may wish to supplement the natural light with a low power flash or with reflected light.

I know of one photographer who is known for his excellence in photographing children. His biggest asset is the woods immediately behind his studio. He merely takes the child for a walk, stays within a given range, and clicks away as the child does interesting things. Nothing is as charming as a natural light shot of a child's fascination with a leaf or flower.

Two difficult conditions you can encounter doing this type of shooting is when you are in shadow and the subject is in strong light or vice versa. You can master either situation by adjusting your f-stop to a more appropriate setting. In an automatic camera, that means either overriding the automatic controls or manually locking the shutter on the subject prior to shooting. This is necessary because of the way an automatic camera reads the light. It's an averaging process. Thus, when both the subject or object and the background to be photographed are under similar conditions, there is no problem with the automatic settings of the camera. When you get into tricky lighting situations, the camera is averaging undesirable as well as desirable light. Sometimes the undesirable light or lack of light upsets the averaging process and your subject is lost in shadow or becomes merely a white blur.

What all that means is you need to "outsmart" the automatic controls on a camera if the predominant light source is not reflected from your subject.

Three ways you can handle this situation are to open up two or three f-stops while holding the speed constant; or hold the camera inches from the subject's face and trip the lever that locks the mechanism. (On my camera, the shutter release button, when half depressed, locks the meter. On other brands, there may be a separate lever for this purpose.) Then, with the mechanism locked, retreat the proper distance and trip the shutter; or as an option you could get in extremely tight so the subject's face fills the frame. This last technique can also create a very desirable halo effect with the subject's backlighted hair—but keep it tight.

Figure 20-4. For a subject with strong backlighting, if you let the automatic camera do your thinking, the background will be light gray and the subject black.

Figure 20-5. Locking the shutter on an automatic camera.

Figure 20-6. Tight framing with strong backlighting.

The reverse situation is when your subject is small and the entire background is dense shadow or black.

Figure 20-7. On an automatic setting, your finished photograph will have a dark gray background and the subject will be a washed-out white blur.

In this situation, the three ways of correcting are to stop down (move to a tighter *f*-stop); or lock the mechanism as we did before; or frame extremely tightly (again, as we did before).

One of the tough shooting assignments I find myself in with training programs is shooting pictures of blacks in white uniforms. It's tough to make both the person and the clothing come out right. Again, the problem is the contrast. The faces would come out too dark or, on the other hand, the clothing would come out dingy gray. Of course, the person's face is the important aspect of the photograph, so I employ the same techniques I use for a person against a strongly lit background, but instead of opening up two or three stops, I would open up only one or two to try to preserve the crispness of the uniform. In situations in which the uniform was not critical to the shot, I would request the people to wear colored clothing.

Some ways to put natural light on the subject. Use reflective surfaces to bounce light onto the subject. By reflective surfaces, I mean anything that does not absorb light. One of the objects you can use is the special photographic umbrellas that are sold for this purpose. You can also use flat pieces of sheet metal. Or, two simple devices you can make yourself are art board painted with metallic paint or with aluminum kitchen foil glued on it. One, two, or three of these can direct reflected light onto your subject as easily and efficiently as spotlights. One very simple trick you can try is to have a seated subject hold a piece of white art board on his or her lap (out of camera range) for a softening of shadows under the chin or jawline. If just a small amount of reflected light is needed, you can do that with almost any light-colored material on location. For example, a newspaper held slightly off camera can light the off-side of a face.

You can extend the range of natural-light photography by fitting your film to the amount of available light, which takes us up to our next topic.

Film Speed

Film, black-and-white or color, comes in a wide range of speeds for different applications and results. The coding for speeds of film is usually stated in ASA* numbers, such as ASA 23, 40, 64, 80, 100 and so on. The higher the ASA number, the less light needed to expose it. Another determining factor in selecting film is the grain of the film. Usually, the faster the speed of the film, the larger the grain will be. Larger-grain films have a tendency to lose ultrafine detail and to give more contrast between lights and darks. The reason I'm staying away from too positive a statement about grain is because film gets better all the time. The range of options is getting broader, too, so from time to time you should check the camera dealers and film processors to see what's new. In addition to film speed and grain, there are special types of film for special applications.

Film Type

The first rule in color photography is, if possible, to match the type of film to the lights you are using. Then select the speed. For instance, for my copystand work,

*American Standards Association.

I use tungsten photo lights and tungsten film. Although in that application I can use any speed film, I prefer to work with a 160-speed E-6 process film. The reason is that particular film also gives me the flexibility for use in other places where I'm using tungsten lights but don't have the intense candle power I have on the copystand. If you can't match the film that way, then use a filter. Fluorescent lights are a problem. Usually they put a green cast on the film. I don't know a specific film that will correct this problem. The technique to consider in this application is to use a color filter keyed to the specific type of film and fluorescent tube in use. The combination that usually works is daylight E-6 film and an FLD filter. If this doesn't work, you may wish to get further consultation from your local camera dealer.

The current range of color slide film is from ASA 25 to ASA 400. If you want absolute detail and are using daylight, you can get excellent detail and color saturation from ASA 25 film. On the other hand, if light is your primary concern, the higher ASA film would better suit your purposes. At a setting of ASA 400, average daylight inside typical buildings or houses is usually adequate.

Pushing It

If you don't have quite enough light to use ASA 400, you can push the film some in processing. Here's the technique for that: Let's say, with your camera set at ASA 400, your meter indicates a 1.8 f-stop. Set the aperture at f4 so you can get some depth, and the film-speed indicator at 1600, and go ahead and shoot. When you take the film for processing, ask the processor to push it two stops. Remember, though, that the whole roll is being pushed, so any frames shot under regular conditions will be overexposed by two stops. Thus, the best policy is to shoot the whole roll at these settings so you have some consistency in the finished product.

Pushing film and shooting at low light levels with a wide open aperture are once-in-a-while tricks you may have to use to fit a particular time and situation. But let's face it—it ain't the ideal way of doing things.

Artificial Lighting

The entire subject of artificial lighting is a science in itself, but a handful of tips can get you consistently good results. That's what I'll try to give you here—a handful of tips. While they may not make you a lighting expert, they should greatly improve your amateur standing.

Two basic types of lighting are electronic flash (strobe) and tungsten. They both work, but within limitations. The trick is picking the right one for your application.

Flash attachments are relatively inexpensive, highly portable, and, if synchronized to your camera, almost foolproof. That's the good side. The not-too-good aspects are that unless used wisely they can rob your photos of depth, turn red the eyes of human subjects, and generally lose background detail. With all that going against them, are they still worth owning? The answer to that is a definite yes. Or, more correctly, yes—but. The "but" is in adding flexibility to the attachment.

One use we already spoke of was a fill light on hazy days. Another way of extending your flash's capability is to take it off the camera and hand hold it at arm's length. Slant the flash slightly downward toward the subject. This is not possible with all cameras. But, if your camera is the type that triggers the flash through a PC cord, it will work. If all you have is a short PC cord, you can buy an extension that will allow you to do this. The result is more depth to your photos. That depth is created because the flash, in this position, will cast light shadows on your subject while "pulling" them out of the background.

One of the best techniques is to bounce light onto your subjects. You need a light-colored or white ceiling to do that.

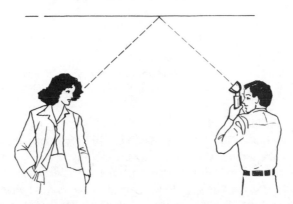

Figure 20-8. Using a flash to bounce light off the ceiling.

The result is a soft fill light similar to the type of daylight on an overcast day. The important thing to remember when you bounce light or hand-hold a flash attachment is that you must set your flash guide number to one that compensates for the full length the light travels. And, as a rule of thumb, open up two f-stops to compensate for the reflected light lost. The fact that the camera is only 6 feet away from the subject means nothing. What counts is that the light is traveling almost twice the distance and, for half of it, it is in a reflected state. The minor adjustment in calculations to get your settings correct is worth the effort.

The price of electronic flash attachments is predicated on output and automatic features and flexibility. Although it's possible to buy a simple unit for $15 to $20, an all-purpose one is a good deal more costly. The cost of these units usually starts at about $90 and goes up from there. If portability and candid or action shots are what you need, they're worth the money.

Photofloods or tungsten lighting require film to match. The advantages of lights over flash-type units are that they permit you to further refine the art of photography. With them, you can create depth and other highlights, and most importantly, they let you see what you're going to get in advance of the shot. The disadvantages are that, although they can be disassembled and packed, they're still bulky and require some setup time and a good source of power. If you are going to do a long series or copystand work, they're the only way to go (unless, of course, you can get natural light).

A simple light setup is two lights. On a copystand, the lights are usually of equal intensity and placed at 45° angles to the subject. The camera is then placed so it shoots into the apex of the 90° corner they create. Studio shots of people or objects are usually lighted in a different manner. The main light source is usually of higher intensity than the fill light. Or, if both lights are of equal intensity, the main light is placed closer to the subject so it projects stronger light on the subject

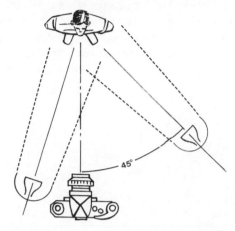

Figure 20-9. Using two lights to photograph people.

than does the fill light. In a two-light setup, the main light is placed at a 45° angle to the subject and the camera, and at a height of 60° or so above the subject. The fill light is placed alongside the camera at a 90° angle to the subject. I say that this is the usual setup because, in certain instances, you may wish to place lights at a shallower angle to reduce glare. In factories where foods are produced, most of the machinery is stainless steel. Lights placed at 45° and 90° can give you undesirable reflected glare. In the instances when we are doing close-up shooting, both lights are placed at 30° angles to the part of the machine being photographed.

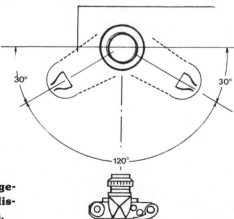

Figure 20-10. This lighting arrangement gives good detail and even distribution of light with no hot spots.

When three lights are used, the arrangement is usually with the first two lights placed as in a two-light setup. A lower-powered one is added to fill the background. The lower-powered light is adjusted so the background does not photograph lighter or darker than the subject. When you are adjusting the intensity of your light setup, you can ensure accuracy by using a Kodak Neutral Testcard. A testcard is just that. It's an 8 x 10 inch card that has been manufactured to reflect 90 percent of light on the white side and 18 percent on the gray side. They cost about $1 and come with an instruction sheet. Using a gray card and a light meter (the one in your camera will do) to measure the illumination, you can meter each light individually and one at a time, making adjustments as you go. In that way, you can get the match desired among the main, fill, and background lights.

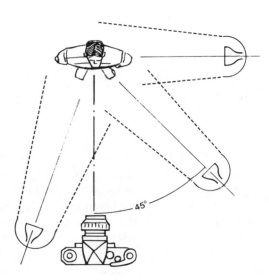

**Figure 20-11.
A three-light setup.**

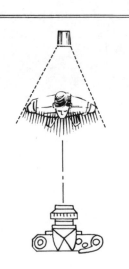

Figure 20-12. Placement of a hair light in a four-light setup.

In some photographic studios, another low-power light with a very thin beam is used as a key light to highlight a portion of the subject's face or hair.

In this common four-light setup, top or hair light is added to create a halo effect of the subject's hair and to "pull" his or her image away from the background. Incidentally, a similar top light is also used to light live speakers at large meetings. The result is the same. It adds a nice glow to the speaker's hair and "pulls" them out of the drapery. The placement of a light for this use is slightly offset behind and several feet above the speaker's head.

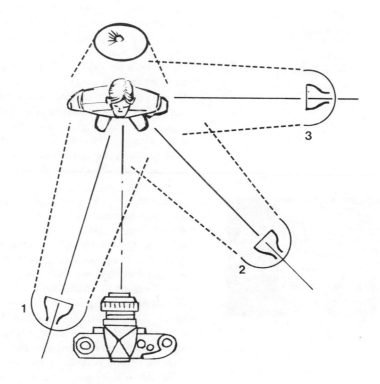

Figure 20-13. A four-light setup using a bare bulb for backlighting.

There is yet another way to give subjects a halo of light. That is with a bare bulb placed directly behind the subject. The body is used to block the light. In the blocking action, the light diffuses around the upper body and creates a complete halo effect. This is a once-in-a-while technique that is used mainly in fashion photography, but you may wish to try it for a specific series of shots.

Special applications of light can also give you ultradramatic product shots. With the right setup, you can float the product center screen with seemingly no background or surround it with a solid black background.

Figure 20-14. You don't have to set-tle for product shots like this.

Figure 20-15. To float the product, a backlighted sheet of milk-white translucent plastic is placed on the sheet and the front lighting is concentrated on the product with no bleed over to cast a shadow on the background. The result is a product floating in mid-air. How much back-lighting is needed will require a little experimenting on your part. The general idea is to get enough light through the plastic to wash out—but not burn out—the background.

Figure 20-16. For a solid black back-ground, construct a backdrop of no-gloss black *velvet*. Black paper reflects light and will appear dark gray. Black rayon will show lines or streaks from the weave of the fabric. Black *velvet* is the only fabric that totally absorbs light and photographs black. The backdrop should be con-structed so there are no sharp angles or wrinkles in the shadow. The front light is concentrated on the product with no bleed over on the back-ground.

Either type of slide can mix well with slides made from flat artwork. Although it's possible to copy flat art in other ways, the preferred method is on a copystand. This one piece of equipment is the mainstay of producing slides for A/V presen-tations.

We'll tell you all about copystands in Chapter 21.

Copystands and
How to Use Them

*He that would have a cake out of the wheat must
tarry the grinding.*

— WILLIAM SHAKESPEARE

A Slide Producer's Best Friend—The Copystand

Complete slide programs can be, and often are, shot in their entirety on a copy-stand. If you are not familiar with the term, it's a catchall to cover a wide range of production equipment used to shoot slides. They can be as simple as a box that holds your camera steady up to very complex and very expensive pieces of equipment. But regardless of how expensive the equipment, the principles stay the same.

Commercially, the stands run from about $70 up to many thousands. And, I have seen a number of home-built ones. Rather than advise you on which type best fits your needs, let me simply state what a camera stand is supposed to do: hold a camera and artwork in fixed positions, level and parallel to one another, in a manner so that the stand does not interfere with either. The stand I use most often is a commercially built one that cost in the neighborhood of $100 about ten years ago. It looks like the illustration at the top of the page.

Any one of my 35mm cameras can be attached. But for reasons we'll discuss later, I do not use the less expensive one on the copystand.

Going up in price of copystands, it's possible to buy pin register setups for artwork, stands that project light guides for lining up art, and stands with automatic focusing. Unless you are planning to go into slide production as a full-time business, your needs are most likely going to be met through a simple stand and two lights. Because, once again, the only thing you need is something that holds the camera and artwork in level and parallel positions with relative ease.

Choosing the Right Stand and Setting It Up

Can you make a copystand? You bet. Maybe not exactly like a commercial one, but one that will do the same thing. If you are interested in building one, your main concerns will be in keeping everything in square and attaching the mast so that there is no wobble or play between it and the bed of the stand.

If you prefer to buy one, visit a good photography store and see what they have. If you don't see what you want on the floor, ask them if you can look up other ones in their suppliers' catalogs.

The initial setup of a copystand requires some time and some fussing around.

It's worth the effort, because once you complete that work, your slide making is reduced to an almost foolproof mechanical process. There is a difference in the amount of setup time based on whether you buy or build the stand, and further differences according to what type of camera lens you are using. Let's start with the steps for setting up a stand with a single-lens reflex camera. Then we can branch out to take in some problem areas.

Use the proper tools. The first rule is to have the proper accessories or tools. Whatever type of stand you use, you can make it more effective with a small level and a large carpenter's square, a macrolens or at least a set of close-up lenses, and commercial grid paper.

The level is used to maintain the parallel positions of the camera and bed of the stand. The square has two uses. First, it is used to make a shooting grid on the bed of the camera stand. The second use is in positioning auxiliary lighting. The commercial grid paper and close-up lenses are to make the actual through-the-lens adjustments in your setup. (The close-up lenses referred to are the type that screw on the front of your existing lens. These are called close-up filters.) After your stand is set up, you'll also need a piece of nonglare glass approximately the same size as the bed of the stand, and a cable release so you can trip the shutter without disturbing the level of the camera.

Setting up a copystand. Finished slides are in a 3 x 2 format. (Standard commercial slide mounts have a viewing area of roughly 34mm x 23mm, but the film scrap inside is 36mm x 24mm.) Our first objective is to translate that format into viewing areas at given distances. Here's where the close-up lenses and grid paper come in. Here are the steps:

- Determine if the bed of the stand is precisely square. If not, correct its position. If it is, go on.

- Find the exact center of the bed of the copystand.

- Fit a piece of photographic grid paper so its center is exactly over the center of the bed. (You can buy this at a photographic store. If none is available, you can build your own grid as you progress through these steps.)

- Using a level, level the bed of the stand.

- Load your camera with film that matches your light source—daylight, tungsten, or whatever.

- Mount the camera to the mast and level it so it is exactly parallel to the bed of the stand. (Each time you move the camera up or down the mast, level it.)

- If you are using auxiliary lighting, position your lights. For flat artwork, position them at 90° to one another and at 45° to the artwork. Your square will help you make this an exact setting.

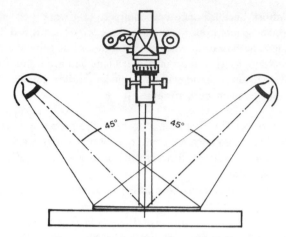

Figure 21-1. Check with a square.

- Mount your *most powerful* close-up lens and focus it at its shortest range on the bed of the stand by moving the camera up or down the mast. Relevel the camera. (If you are not using grid paper, you'll need to make a reference mark to assist you in focusing.) When you have your focus and distance correct, mark your field of vision on the bed and make a corresponding mark on the mast. For quick visual references, you may wish to do this with a simple color code or numerical code.

- Now work your camera up the mast using, in succession, your weaker close-up lenses, then just straight lenses. Continue to make reference marks so you can handle four or five various sizes of artwork.

- When you have finished your marking procedure, your stand should look something like this:

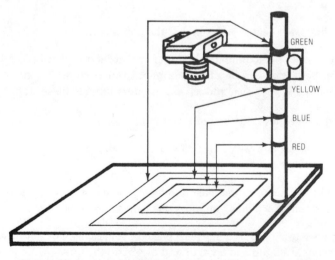

Figure 21-2. A copystand setup for slide production.

These are the instructions for a single-lens reflex or a camera that otherwise focuses through the lens. These are the only types of cameras recommended for copystands. Cameras that focus through a separate aperture are not recommended because of the variance between the focusing aperture and the lens. This is called parallax. The closer to the work you hold that type of camera, the greater the problem. Here's how that works:

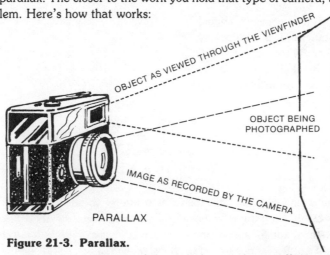

Figure 21-3. Parallax.

As you can see, when you get close enough to make an effective slide, you'll crop the top edge from the artwork. For that reason, I don't recommend rangefinder cameras for copystand work. It's just too much by "guess and by golly" to get consistently good results. However, if that's the kind of camera you have and you want to use it on a copystand, there's an extremely good explanation for doing so in the book: *Planning and Producing Audiovisual Materials,* Jerrold E. Kemp, Chandler Publishing Company, Scranton, PA, 1968. Incidentally, this is an extremely good all-around reference book for your library.

Correcting White Backgrounds

With reference marks in place and everything level, you're ready to attach your cable release and shoot a test roll. Production slides, generally, do not have white backgrounds. The reasons are that it is too hard to control exposures and they are usually not very attractive when projected. One of the ways you can correct white backgrounds is to place a gel (transparent sheet of colored plastic) over the artwork. For most accurate results, meter your light with the gray card mentioned earlier and set your camera to that reading. Most colors will come out to the proper shades. If you are shooting a white grid, you may wish to use a gel for your test rolls to assist in exposure readings. The gel is flattened and weighted with a piece of nonglare glass approximately the same dimensions as the bed of the stand. As you'll see later, you'll use this piece of nonglare glass in other applications on the copystand. An important point to remember when buying the glass is to have the edges polished. For additional protection against cuts or breakage, tape the edges of the glass.

Reference Sheets

You'll need to make a reference sheet so you can check your results against your various camera settings. A reference sheet should include distances and *f*-stops by frame number. When you're shooting test rolls, bracket your *f*-stops by shooting three frames at each position.

TEST ROLL #			DATE		
Frame #	F-Stop	Distance	Frame #	F-Stop	Distance
1			19		
2			20		
3			21		
4			22		
5			23		
6			24		
7			25		
8			26		
9			27		
10			28		
11			29		
12			30		
13			31		
14			32		
15			33		
16			34		
17			35		
18			36		

Figure 21-4. Sample reference sheet.

When you're shooting test rolls (or for that matter, production shots), bracket your *f*-stops by shooting three frames of the same subject: one at an *f*-stop below your light meter reading, one on, and one over. If your camera has half stops, you may wish to shoot five exposures at each distance on a test roll—one below, one-half below, right on, one-half over, and one over. When you have completed your chart, it should look like one of these:

TEST ROLL # /		DATE 11/19			
Frame #	F-Stop	Distance	Frame #	F-Stop	Distance
1	F4	Red	19		
2	F5.6	Red	20		
3	F8	Red	21		
4	F4	Blue	22		
5	F5.6	Blue	23		
6	F8	Blue	24		
7			25		
8			26		
9			27		
10			28		
11			29		
12			30		
13			31		
14			32		
15			33		
16			34		
17			35		
18			36		

Figure 21-5. Whole stops.

TEST ROLL # /		DATE 11/19			
Frame #	F-Stop	Distance	Frame #	F-Stop	Distance
1	F4	Red	19		
2	F4+½	Red	20		–
3	F5.6	Red	21		
4	F5.6+½	Red	22		
5	F8	Red	23		
6	F4	Blue	24		
7	F4+½	Blue	25		
8	F5.6	Blue	26		
9	F5.6+½	Blue	27		
10	F8	Blue	28		
11			29		
12			30		
13			31		
14			32		
15			33		
16			34		
17			35		
18			36		

Figure 21-6. Half stops.

When you take your test rolls in for processing, be sure to ask the processor to number each slide sequentially (some do not do this automatically).

When your slides are returned, be sure to put all of them in the correct sequence by frame number, then check them against your reference sheets. Two major variations from normal that you should look for are exposure and any blurring or falling off of lines around or near the edges of the grid. If there is an exposure deficiency of more than one full stop, you may wish to have the camera checked. If there is any fall-off (lines becoming faint or twisted) around one of the edges of the test frame, you should have that checked. If you have either problem and are going to get the camera checked, it will help to take the test slides with you to show the dealer.

As I said earlier, it takes a little time and fussing around to get your camera stand set up correctly. But look at that time as an investment. Because from this point on, your shooting can be a quick, almost automatic procedure with few foul-ups. The key to remember is to level your camera each time you mount it or move it on the mast.

Guarding Against Reflections

There is one more situation you should be aware of—picking up reflections of your camera in the nonglare glass used to keep the artwork flat. Correct placement of the lights (90°) usually eliminates this problem, but if it doesn't, then mask the camera with black felt or velvet. Roughly construct a sack with the black material and masking tape so only the lens and the controls protrude.

FELT MASK

NONGLARE GLASS

Figure 21-7. Use a felt mask and nonglare glass to avoid reflections.

Now, with everything set up, it's merely a matter of placing correctly formatted art on the bed of the stand, weighting it with nonglare glass, and shooting. You can work your way through a pretty hefty stack of artwork in one afternoon of shooting. All that's needed now is the artwork.

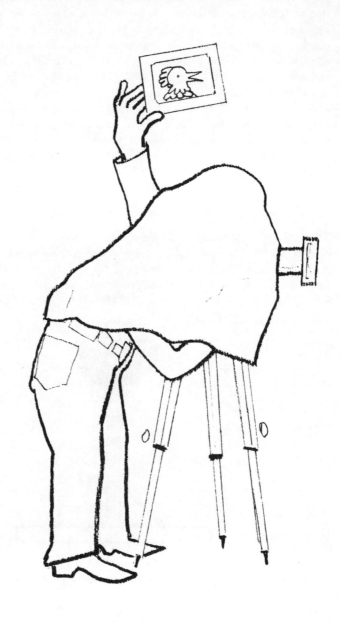

Some Advanced
Techniques for Slide
Preparation

*A little learning is not a dangerous thing to one who
does not mistake it for a great deal.*

—WILLIAM ALLEN WHITE

Artwork for Slides

All of the materials we discussed earlier in overhead transparencies will work in preparing artwork for slides. Most of the techniques will, too. One important exception is the "reveal" that we showed. In slide production, instead of a reveal, we use a series called a "build." I'll show you how to do this in this chapter, as well as introduce other techniques.

There are some additional materials and techniques you should consider:

Materials	*Techniques*	
Existing photos	Single thoughts	Builds
3-D Lettering	Big, bold symbols	Sequences
Color	Vivid colors	

Materials

Existing photos are excellent. One precaution is that you familiarize yourself with the copyright laws so you do not infringe upon someone's right by copying everything in sight. Magazines; newspapers; travel, cultural, art, and history books are all good sources for pictures. These can usually be shot on the copystand without removing the page from the book.

I've known people who made slides of ancestors from photos in their family album. These worked out well when a "period" or "place" piece was being produced. One person I know recently borrowed his grandmother's photo album, reshot everything on the copystand, and had ten sets of dupes made. They made meaningful Christmas gifts to brothers and sisters and cousins—and at a reasonable price. You'll notice that, when copying existing photos, the formats are different. In other words, if you get the whole length in, you are not going to get the entire breadth. That looks rather tacky with two borders showing. To compensate for that, focus inside all the borders so none show in the finished slide. When producing slides, photographs will be helped by this technique because most of them have too much background. Good slides, in most instances, are big and bold.

Three-D lettering is used mainly in titling or to add weight to an idea. The letters come in a variety of typefaces and materials. Some of the materials are magnetic rubber, plaster, plastic, and ceramic. Their main purposes are to provide depth, weight, and reusability.

Figure 22-1. (*a*) The third side of the letters catch the light. (*b*) That, in turn, creates depth ... (*c*) through shadows. Make these shadows work for you through correct placement of lights. If more shadow is desired, widen the angle between your two copystand lights. If shadow is desired on one side only, use both lights on the opposite side of the letters. Each time you change the lighting, the depth and the mood of the lettering changes. If you buy this type of lettering, you may wish to shoot a couple of test rolls of film to experiment with various effects you can create.

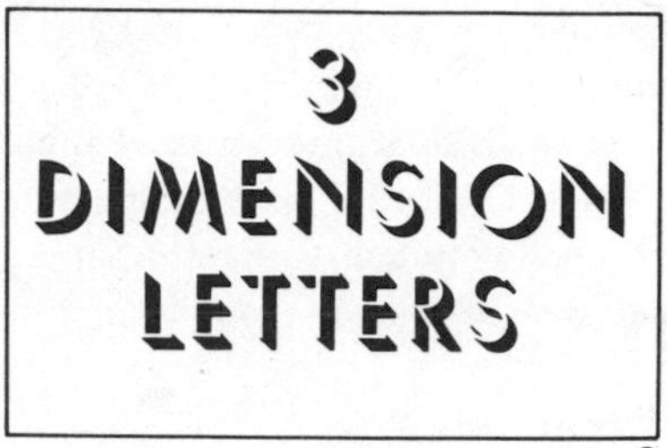

3
DIMENSION
LETTERS

a

CREATE
DEPTH

b

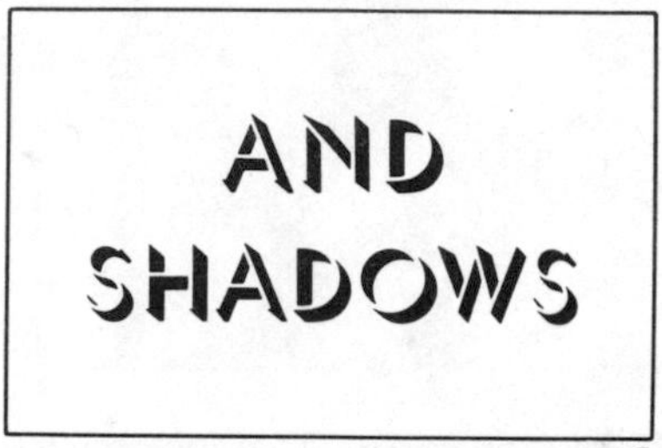

AND
SHADOWS

c

A young friend of mine, Burt Wolder of AT&T, created a truly magnificent catalog cover through photoreproduction of 3-D lettering. He used it to set the title over a background photograph. I've always admired that cover. Burt's idea is one you can store away in your bag of tricks to use at some future date for a different type project.

Using color for effect. Color can work for you or—if not used wisely—against you. Muted colors near the center of a gray scale in intensity can give a harmonious effect when used together. On the other hand, colors directly opposite on a color wheel (complementary colors), such as yellow and purple, can be discordant. Sometimes that is what you want to create—the effects of chaos, explosion, discordance, opposition, and so on.

Generally, the colors are chosen close but not next to each other on a color wheel. For instance, red and yellow opposed to red and orange or orange and yellow. Pure colors are preferred. Try to stay away from ones that are too muted or have a muddy look. Used correctly, colors tie the slide together and complement the message and the symbol shown.

A good idea may be to change the background color of slides as the topics change. On the other hand, it's usually poor technique to alternate from one background to another within the same subtopic. The exception is when you intentionally wish to create some visual disharmony to make a point.

Techniques

Single ideas are expressed on individual slides. There should be instant recognition of what is being shown and what it means. Audiences are not going to work too hard to get your message. Too much detail is just plain boring. Multiple ideas are handled through builds and sequences of slides. In some instances, single thoughts can be broken down into multiple images.

Big and bold is what makes an impression. Usually that means filling the screen with the image and leaving only as much background as is necessary for emphasis or to tell the story. The only precautions are not to give your slides a consistently crowded look or to create an imbalance in the design. If in some instances that means dropping off part of the subject, don't be afraid to do it. It works.

Let's draw a couple of examples. I think you'll agree that big and bold is best.

Figure 22-2. Big is better. (*a*) These women are not engaged in any activity that adds to the viewers' understanding. Therefore, the interest is in their faces. (*b*) By cropping closer, some of the background clutter is lost and the slide becomes more interesting. (*c*) Here all attention is focused where it should be—on their faces. Individual subjects can be framed even tighter for more dramatic results: (*d*) horizontal, and (*e*) vertical.

d

e

How to build a "build." A "build" is the slide equivalent of the "reveal" overhead transparency. In its simplest form, it's the process of adding lines of type to a series of sequential slides. Two basic examples we can use are from the overhead cells in Figures 17-3 and 17-7. Here's how each of them can be transformed into slide builds.

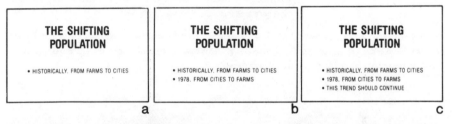

Figure 22-3. Build No. 1. This is the same material we presented in Figure 17-3 as an overhead transparency reveal, now shown in slide format. All three slides need to be accompanied by appropriate narration.

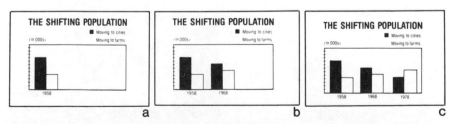

Figure 22-4. Build No. 2. A graph, such as the one we used earlier, can be built in multiple steps so the speaker can hold back the surprise of what happens until the "right" moment to get the desired impact. This example is a direct translation to slides of the overhead transparency presented in Figure 17-7.

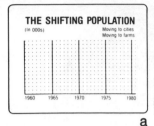

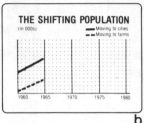

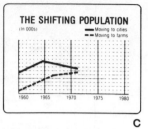

a   b   c

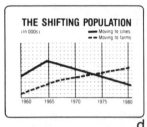

d

Figure 22-5. Build No. 3. Going a step further, we can take the graph shown as an overhead cell in Figure 17-4 and create a slightly different kind of build. In this one, all the slides have the same background, and the graph lines lengthen in successive order as they fit the narrative. For more dramatic results, alternate the slides between two projectors working from a common dissolve unit. If you go this route, all slides need to be in perfect registration so there is no fuzziness when there is an overlap. Another two-projector technique is to have the graph background in one slide machine and lines only on slides in another projector. Make the lines grow through slide changes in the second projector while projector one remains static on the graph background.

Special note: All sequential slides in any of the builds shown can be shot from a single piece of artwork by shooting, adding artwork, shooting, adding art, and repeating as many times as necessary.

Figure 22-6. Simple sequences visually unfold a story. In one such as this, no words are needed. The fourth slide's layout, which can be in chaotic colors, adds to the effect. The final touch is adding an appropriate sound effect timed to the last slide.

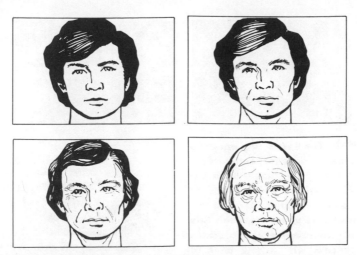

Figure 22-7. Earlier in the book, I talked about visibly aging a person with slides as their life story was told. In the real sequence, more frames were used but four will work. The tricky part is keeping every photo in perfect registration. The image on all slides, whether shot from art or photographs, has to be the same size and in the same position on the film. Additionally, care must be taken so each piece of film is similarly positioned within the mounts. The preferred way of projecting these is from two projectors working in tandem with a dissolve unit. The secondary method is with quick cuts between two projectors.

Sequences. Sequences are similar to builds in that, in themselves, they tell a story. Sometimes that is a single thought built from jigsaw scraps. Sequences can also be worked in reverse to carry your thoughts from the large to the small by narrowing your attention by degrees.

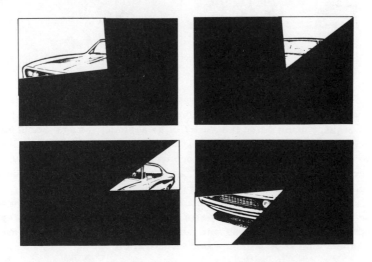

Figure 22-8. The jigsaw sequence. To build dramatic suspense, some items may be revealed piecemeal or in jigsaw fashion. Often, these types of sequences are set to music to add further interest. As you go through this series, try to imagine these slides falling successively on the beat of  rapid music with the complete object timed to hit the screen accompanied by a cymbal clash or other audio punctuation. If you need impact, this is one way to get it!

Figure 22-9. The narrowing process is a sequence in which the audience's attention is directed to increasingly smaller detail. With this technique, you are doing the work for the audience (as you should be). Everything is completely visible at all times. Here's how that might work: "When the drilling° ends, each wellhead is equipped with what is known, in the field vernacular°, as a 'Christmas tree.' At the base is one of our valves.° You'll notice that this particular type valve . . ." As you can see, it would only be a short leap to narrow this down to one or more of the internal parts of the valve. The entire process takes only a few seconds and simplifies what may have forever remained a mystery without good visualization.

The process of sequencing becomes almost endless, but you can use these four different approaches as thought starters.

Your imagination should be off and running on ways you can individualize these techniques to fit your needs. One last thought on this subject is a product of a friend's creativity. It's such a clever idea that I want you to see it. Who knows—you may be able to put it to work for yourself.

Clem Roether is a truly great A/V scriptwriter and program producer. In past years I have had the pleasure of working with Clem on a number of major A/V shows. One of the ideas Clem came up with during one of these shows was a creative way to introduce a child-oriented product to a sales force. Here's what he did to get the point across. He and his partner at the time, Jim Shattuck, had all of the art drawn in a childish scrawl with crayons on blue-lined school paper, then photographed it into slides. The narrative was a tape of children endorsing the product. The results were excellent. The art was clear, the message simple, and the style matched the message. What could be better than that! Not much, because all of the key points of A/V artwork were covered. They're also the points you should remember—clarity of message, legibility of artwork, and compatibility with the style of the speaker and other visuals.

Just for fun and to stretch our imaginations, let's look at how that little stick figure sequence got the message across.

Figure 22-10. Matching the visual to the message through the use of cartoon characters.

Summing Up

It is better to be always upon your guard, than to suffer once.

—LATIN PROVERB

Murphy Was an Optimist (Corollary to Murphy's Law)

Our intention in writing this book was to make it the most *practical* book on the subject, with just enough theory to fill the needs of our do-it-yourself readers. Accordingly, we wrote the first draft with a minimum of consultation of existing books on the subject. (Although, between us, we think we have probably read most of the good ones.) Everything we put down on paper came straight from our own experiences.

Once the first draft was complete, we felt it was time to check the literature to make sure we hadn't left out anything vital. At the same time, we began compiling our bibliography. Both of us assembled individual lists of the books and publications we thought to be valuable; then we asked Ms. Mary Raitt, a professional researcher, to perform an independent search. The result is that we have now what we believe to be the most complete and up-to-date bibliography ever assembled in a book of this size and scope.

We have also spot-checked many books we had read in the past, to remind ourselves of subject areas we had inadvertently overlooked. This research disclosed that we had indeed omitted some vital information. Public happenings and news stories also brought some important points to our attention. For example, while we were working on our revisions, a terrible hotel fire disaster took place in Las Vegas—reminding us to mention fire safety in our book and furnish a source for additional information on the subject.

Similarly, recent waves of terrorism have reminded us to write about security measures. You'll find discussions of both, plus a number of otherwise unmentioned items, in this wrap-up chapter.

We also discovered that, as we began to summarize, reinforce, and add new tidbits, what we were really doing was writing a chapter on troubleshooting. Maybe that's the best way to end this book anyway—because there will inevitably be some occurrence that you didn't plan for in your meeting. This chapter contains tips that will help you prevent a few of those from happening.

Murphy's Law says that anything that can go wrong will. Even allowing for exaggeration, you'll quickly gain respect for his idea when you're trying to put on a first-class meeting.

There are ways of beating the law—plan for trouble and predetermine what you are going to do when it strikes. Believe it or not, most problems that occur in association with meetings are predictable.

That's the reason experienced meeting planners learn to avoid trouble by taking precautionary steps before the fact. And, to ensure that they've touched all bases, they follow a checklist for each set of instances to guide them through the maze of possible problems and their avoidance.

Rather than present you with a single checklist to fit every possible occurrence, we'll furnish the material you'll need to generate your own. Requirements change from one meeting to the next; so should your checklist. Here are some common problems that can either be avoided or quickly solved through a little advance planning. The type of meeting you are conducting should determine which of these find their way onto your checklist.

Trouble—Even Before Arriving at the Meeting Site

Hotel reservations. On your first contact with the hotel, be sure to (a) designate the number of rooms and (b) agree upon a plus/minus figure. As closely as possible, break these figures out by types of accommodations. For instance, 3 executive suites, 15 small suites, 100 double rooms, 30 single rooms, and a percent of over/under leeway on the double and single rooms.

One word of caution! On meetings of this size (medium), it would be wise to make your reservations up to a year in advance. (Extremely large meetings or conventions are sometimes booked *three or more* years in advance.) With smaller meetings, you can book on much shorter notice.

Meeting rooms should also be designated—and booked—with a clear understanding that you will need the meeting rooms a certain number of hours or days in advance of the actual affair. This time frame should closely correspond to the actual time you need to set up the stage and equipment, plus an allowance for rehearsal time.

Three main problems can occur with hotels: First, the sleeping room reservations and meeting room reservations are often handled by two totally separate departments of the hotel. There may be communication problems between these departments. If that's the case, the big loser could be you.

The second problem is that hotels are often unwilling to book meeting rooms several days in advance of the affair because rooms being used for rehearsal are not producing revenue.

The third problem is that a large meeting may be already booked and scheduled to end a day or so before yours is to begin. If this group does not clear the premises on schedule (and this often happens), you are going to be delayed in your preparations. Your solution? If you find, when you are booking your meeting, that a large meeting is preceding yours, postpone your meeting for a day or two.

While you should respect the hotel's situation, you still need to guard your own interests so as to enable adequate preparation for your own meeting.

Here are some ways of dealing with these problems *before* they can happen: First, for large meetings, when dealing with the hotel, make certain that the person in charge of booking meeting rooms—as well as the sales manager—is in on your conversations. Then make it a firm point to negotiate time needed for room setup. When this is agreed upon, put it in writing. Do the same with sleeping room arrangements. You may wish to include a penalty clause in your contract that would take effect in the event the hotel cannot produce the rooms as agreed upon. This would be particularly true if they insist on a penalty if *you* default.

Second, as you get closer to the meeting time, *be sure to periodically reconfirm* all of your plans with *all* involved persons.

Keep in mind, when reconfirming plans, that hotel personnel may change; you could end up dealing with a new person or persons. You'll need to fill them in on your plans and bring them up to date.

Third, confirm the exact number of hotel rooms needed, by type, as early as possible in the game. As meeting time nears, furnish the hotel a list, by name, of the people attending, and note the type of accommodation that each person will need. If you are asking the hotel to preregister guests, you or a designee will want to check the preregistration cards against your list, and assist with the actual room assignments. For extremely large meetings, this is essential. Only you know, for reasons of courtesy, health, handicap, or security, who goes where.

Travel reservations. On small- to medium-size meetings, the best plan usually is to have the proposed attendees make their own travel arrangements. They will then need to notify you of their exact arrival time far enough in advance so that you can convey this information to the hotel.

For large meetings, an organization may plan the travel arrangements for each attendee. It may do this through a travel agency or through a designated person within the organization. Either way, tickets have to be sent to attendees far enough in advance to permit making any needed adjustments and notifying the organization of the new plan. The beauty of having the organization plan everyone's travel is that, for reasons of status or security, people can be combined into ideal travel groups.

Scripts and visuals—don't lose them! If you are conducting a small seminar or meeting, *you* should be in charge of your own scripts and visuals. For larger meetings, the *leader* should be charged with the responsibility. With extremely large groups, the *meeting planner* or *coordinator* should be assigned the task. The master script book should stay in the hands of this one person.

For small meetings, only a few simple procedures are needed. The key factor is to keep the script and visuals on your person. This becomes particularly important when traveling. The script, visuals, and all handouts or exercises that are important to the success of your meeting go in the passenger compartment of the plane with you. Other material, such as handouts or workbooks for the attendees, can be checked as luggage, but you'd better hedge this bet, too! Keep *one copy* of the whole bundle on your person, and if the meeting is in Peoria and your bags are in Honolulu, you can still save the situation. Locate the nearest copy machine, buy covers from the local stationer, and remake the workbooks or handouts. They may not be quite so sharp looking as the ones you lost, but the meeting can still go on.

Handling the master script book for large meetings is fraught with other dangers. Of course, the ever-present one we spoke about of losing it is still there. But there's an even greater hazard—you'll find out what real trouble is if your script book gets into disarray or out of synchronization with the script books used by the technicians in the director's booth or backstage. How do these things happen? Generally, a speaker or someone else connected with the program will make script changes, but somehow the revisions get in only one book.

Here's a procedure to prevent this confusion. Make it a rule that all script changes—intended and real—are to be discussed only with the meeting planner or the show director. Then, the person charged with the responsibility of the master script book will insert and delete copy as required. At the end of each day, he or she will copy the new pages and bring up to date all the books of everyone concerned with the meeting.

With major meetings, you need to observe even more elaborate procedures. In such cases, it is usually not possible for the meeting planner to carry all the visuals, particularly when slides have to be transported a long distance by airplanes. Some of the precautions that major production companies routinely take follow.

Typically, they make *two* copies of every slide. One complete set goes on the plane with the show or stage director; the other set goes on a different plane with the meeting planner, leader, or coordinator. In that way, they are assured that if one set gets lost, the other one has a high probability of arriving at the meeting site in time for rehearsals.

Some companies even further hedge this bet by making *three* copies—the two just mentioned, plus a third that is carried to the meeting site by a trusted ally.

Trouble—During Setup, Rehearsal, or (Gulp!) the Meeting Itself

Unionized meeting or convention facilities. We know some meeting planners who refuse to take a major convention into a property where the help belongs to an organized bargaining unit. In our opinion, this approach is too narrow. The facility may be exactly the one for your meeting—the fact that the employees are organized may have little or no bearing on the situation.

In all honesty, I (Jim) have to say that I've been stung a couple of times by enforcement of a local contract. For instance, on one occasion I was required to hire a projectionist for half a day because, as a speaker, I was going to use four overhead transparencies in a thirty-minute presentation. I had originally planned to put these on the machine myself. No soap. I was "endangering" someone's job.

Our friend Lee Beckner, drawing on his broad experience in the business, furnished us an additional thought on the subject. He once felt the bite of a labor agreement because his room setup took place on Sunday—a day of double-time for all employees. It was passed along to him by the hotel, with no warning.

At the other end of the scale, I've worked on properties where the fact that the employees had a tight union actually worked in my favor. The help was professional and carried out their jobs extremely efficiently. In the long run, the cost was no higher, and their professionalism made my life much easier.

Knowing whether or not a facility is unionized should be Standard Operating Procedure (SOP) for any meeting planner. But the real issues to consider are: How does this affect you? What can you do for yourself? What must they do? How well will they do it? What problems could you encounter? What are the solutions? What is the best working arrangement?

The best way to get these answers is to talk to someone (and, if possible, several persons) who have had similar meetings on the same property. With the answers you get, you can base your choice on logic, not guesswork—just the way you should make all your choices.

Equipment failure. Plan on some malfunctions. For small meetings, merely being equipped to replace the light bulb in a slide projector or overhead projector, or to free a jammed slide tray, is adequate.

Large meetings, once again, are a different story. For multimedia presentations, preparing for malfunction is quite a sizable task. How sizable depends on how much electronic equipment is used in the show. In this particular case, let me go to the far extreme of preparation, and then you can work back and find the happy middle ground for your meeting.

On large multimedia shows, there may be nine to fifteen (or more) 35mm projectors, one or two 16mm projectors, light generators, and other equipment in the system. Even though this is a ton of gear, some meeting producers go so far as to set up an auxiliary branching on their programmers, and completely duplicate the entire backstage system. During the show, the auxiliary machines are turned on and run in tandem with the primary equipment. To keep the auxiliary light beams off the screen, the operators use two-sided boxes with trapdoors on the front. Should a projector in the primary system fail, the operator merely drops the auxiliary trapdoor, and the secondary system continues the show without losing a beat.

Here's one last emergency technique we'd like to share with you: how to quickly change a burned-out light bulb in a 35mm slide projector. Since the machine is hot, the bulb is hot, and there is limited work space, unplug the machine from the electricity; break the bulb by striking it with a pair of pliers (if you have room, you can put a small bag over the bulb to catch the glass and to protect your eyes); seize the base of the bulb with the pliers and extract it from the machine; place the new bulb in the machine with a protective covering (such as a soft cotton glove) over your hand, or use the paper provided inside the light-bulb container. The purpose of the protective covering is to stop body oils on hands from collecting on the surface of the bulb. These cause the light to concentrate, creating a hot spot. These hot spots can burn out the bulb quickly.

Supplies. Although you may ask the hotel to provide you with certain supplies, such as writing tablets, pencils, marking pens, and so on, it behooves you to carry an assortment of these with you in your meeting kit or briefcase—particularly felt-tip markers in a variety of sizes and colors.

One additional suggestion: Make sure you know where the hotel's copying machine is located (or the nearest one in the vicinity if the hotel doesn't have one). You may need to make last-minute copies of additional or supplemental materials. It's not a bad idea also to look up a drug store, stationer, dime store, or such, in the immediate area of the meeting place. Then, if necessary, you can buy additional writing tablets, legal pads, or pencils.

The "meeting kit." Often it's a long, if not fruitless, wait for a hotel maintenance man to perform simple repairs. Extension cords seem particularly hard to locate. And yet they can be among your most essential items of equipment. To guard against a possibly disastrous time lag, you should prepare yourself to be as self-sufficient as possible. That means carrying a "meeting kit."

The size of the kit and what it contains is predicated once again on the size of the meeting. What would be adequate for a small meeting would not be enough equipment for a large meeting.

In a standard meeting kit for a small seminar (one or two speakers), you should carry at least:

- A heavy-duty extension cord
- An adapter plug to go from three-prong plugs into a two-hole electrical socket
- An assortment of felt-tip markers (ranging from very narrow to very wide, in a good range of colors)
- Sign cards
- Blank slides in mounts (in a pinch, you could write or draw on them)
- Pliers
- A screwdriver
- A staple gun and desk stapler
- Wide duct tape to tape cords down to the rug or floor
- A box of push pins
- One or more rolls of masking tape

The kit for large shows contains everything already mentioned, but with items in much larger quantities. It should be supplemented with a specialized mechanic's tool kit. The large meeting kit should contain:

- A heavy-duty stapler
- An assortment of nails
- Thumbtacks
- Push pins

- A hammer
- Several sizes of pliers
- An assortment of screwdrivers
- A wide assortment of electronic plugs to adapt one machine to the other, or to tie two dissimilar cords together
- A wide variety of sizes and types of tape
- An art knife
- A soldering iron and solder
- A selection of solderless electrical connections

Again, if you plan to use a facility you haven't been in before, be sure to check in advance with the hotel to find out whether their help is unionized. If so, you'll want to ask how much of this self-help you can do without violating the hotel's agreement with the union. Some hotel unions couldn't care less; others will not allow you to so much as plug in a slide projector yourself.

For extremely large meetings and multimedia shows, in addition to your own kits, your lead technician may want to carry his own tool kit with specialized wrenches, screwdrivers, fittings, electronic adapters, and any other supplies that conceivably might be used backstage in setting up equipment.

A last-minute checklist for your meeting room. A disorderly or uncomfortable room can kill your meeting. Don't chance it. After you think everything is right, make one more last-minute check:

- Air conditioning or heat at proper level
- Lights working and set at proper intensity
- Tables and/or chairs set up according to plan
- Exit signs lighted and visible, and egresses clear
- Announcement signs in place to guide attendees to meeting rooms
- Room neat
- Smoking and no smoking sections clearly marked
- Ashtrays available where needed
- *All electrical equipment cords taped down*

A last-minute equipment and backstage check. Don't wait until the last minute to check all equipment, which should have already been technically checked for correct operation. But do double-check the following items at the last minute:

- 35mm slide projector
  —bulb and fan working

—spare bulb close at hand
—image focused, exactly filling screen
—tray cued to slot one
—an opaque or pleasant color slide in hole one (to avoid light flash on screen)
- Overhead projector
    —bulb and fan working
    —spare bulb close at hand
    —image focused, filling screen with no "keystoning"
    —first transparency in place on the machine
- Movie projector
    —bulb working
    —image focused and set to fill screen exactly
    —sound set at proper level
    —film cued up to within a few frames of the film title (so the audience doesn't have to watch the entire film leader)
- Music—check playback unit
    —threaded and cued
    —sound set at proper level
    —music on or ready to be turned on as audience enters room
- Lectern
    —reading light on, if appropriate
    —scripts in place
    —spots or backlights positioned
    —each speaker in place at the spot from which he or she will enter the stage
    —each speaker given a last-minute reminder of his or her entrance
    —each person's script in place
    —*all electronic cords securely taped down.*

Using the preceding material and the checklists furnished in Chapter 2 as thought starters, you should have enough material to develop any checklists you wish. Let us emphasize that it is of the utmost importance that you *do* make the checklists (one person can't remember everything)—and use them faithfully.

Security. Unfortunately, we live in a time of terrorist activity. There are many more bomb threats, extortion attempts, and robberies than ever reach the ears of the general public. And, while not of epidemic proportions, there are enough to make it prudent for meeting planners to take certain precautions. Such precautions grow in importance with the size of the get-together and the number of high-ranking dignitaries in attendance.

For small meetings, perhaps you won't need to do anything about security. Large meetings are a different story. Preparing for these may require quite a bit of planning time to ensure the safety of your guests.

If your organization has a security person, it is good sense to enlist his or her help. Some items to consider are:

- What are the hotel's usual guest security measures?

- What is the fire protection in the hotel? (*Meeting News* has a fire safety checklist which it will send out on request. You may write to the editor at Gralla Publications, 1515 Broadway, New York, New York 10036.)

- What are the evacuation procedures?

- Who in the local police force is your contact in case of an extortion or kidnap threat?
- What special precautions are used by hotel personnel or the local police force to ensure the safety of high-ranking dignitaries?
- What is the hotel's procedure if and when they receive bomb threats?
- Is there an organized search team at the hotel?
- What role do the local police play in bomb threats?
- What are the evacuation procedures?
- How and where do you hire an extra guard or guards to watch electronic equipment when the meeting room is not in use; or guards to check the credentials of persons entering the exhibit hall or main meeting room?

This is not an all-inclusive list. If you are conducting an extremely large meeting, take along your organization's security person. He or she can work out the details in advance with the hotel's security force and the local police.

Accidents, illnesses, and personal injury. When a thousand or more people get together in one place at one time, the odds are high that more than one will have an acute physical problem. Each day the conference runs, the likelihood increases. Plan ahead and know what you will be able to do when this occurs. You should determine:
- The availability of the nearest doctor.
- How ambulances are called.
    - —What is the response time?
    - —How are they equipped?
    - —Do you need to hire one to stand by because of slow response time?
- Who at the hotel or in your organization is trained in first aid or CPR?
- Where is the nearest hospital?
- Where is the best nearby hospital for serious medical problems?

Programs for Spouses—No Trouble, Just Opportunity

In past years, it was popular to set up flower shows, tours, and fashion shows for spouses—and such programs went over just fine. But times have changed, and "spouse" no longer just means "wife." There will probably be some male spouses, too. With these changing times and conditions, tours still have appeal, but many of the other so-called traditional programs have gone by the boards. Generally, spouses—whether women or men—are interested these days in learning something more useful. And who can blame them for wanting programs with more "meat" than how to arrange flowers or learn about the latest height of the hemline or depth of the neckline.

With these thoughts in mind, you can program more successfully for spouses if you plan a program around useful, informative, or motivational subjects. Perhaps you can plan a miniseminar about transactional analysis, interpersonal relationships, communications skills, stress, or assertiveness.

Another consideration is that spouses may wish, or actually need, to learn more about the operation of the company itself.

If possible, you may want to include spouses in all the general meeting sessions of the convention, so that they can be better informed about the company as a whole, and what the company hopes to accomplish as a result of the convention. After all, many of the decisions unveiled at meetings and conventions directly affect their lives. Clearly, such items are bound to be of great interest to them.

As a final thought, and one we've seen successfully practiced, consider programs concerning the mechanics of company-sponsored programs that aid the entire family: insurance, vacation, retirement, and other paid benefits.

Trouble—Real-Life Adventures (or, There's a Moral to All Our Stories)

Ambiance. Meetings are only one form of communication. And, while they are fun, they can require a lot of time, work, and usually out-of-pocket cash. If, in spite of this, you decide that is your best way to go, then get the most for your money—by making every aspect of the meeting contribute to its overall success. This requires a firm understanding of an exact objective and a step-by-step plan for reaching it.

Ambiance is a major consideration. The room, overall property, and food service can either add to or detract from what you wish to accomplish. It's the gift wrapping on your presentation.

Plain brown paper may be the best; if it is, do your meeting that way. If, on the other hand, a fancier package is desired, know what you want, what it will do for you, and communicate those plans to everyone involved—which brings us to a real story about ambiance and communication.

Food selection and Murphy's Law. Communication breakdowns are bad enough when everybody speaks the same language. Here's what can happen when one of the participants speaks little English. Don't let it happen to you.

Once, a corporate vice president we know asked his secretary to make all necessary arrangements for a sit-down dinner for thirty persons. He wanted it to be a grand affair, so he asked his secretary to make sure that the main dish was "something out of the ordinary—something truly unusual." He ended his request with, " . . . and use your own discretion."

The instructions seemed clear—and they were—until the secretary reached the French restaurant to make dinner arrangements. She passed along the instructions as well as she possibly could—considering that she spoke no French and the chef spoke no English. But, with accompanying gestures, he assured her everything would be "très magnifique."

The time for the great occasion arrived, and visually, everything the chef had promised seemed to be "superbe." The menu was printed in French; the candles cast a warm glow on the silver and the immaculate linen of the table settings. As the beaming chef had promised, everything was beautiful . . . until dinner was served.

The appetizers were strange, but palatable. The wine was first rate, and the guests sat back waiting for the main course with the greatest anticipation. Then, with great fanfare, another strange dish was brought out by the waiters—a very small crêpe with a chopped meat sauce. To put it delicately, it was a kind of French version of an old Army favorite politely described as chipped beef on toast. The guests assumed it was another of the hors d'ouevres, but most of them ate it. It had, after all, been a long day; the hour was late, and everyone was ravenous. That was enough to tide them over while they waited for the main course to arrive.

Then, with flourishes, a flaming dessert was served.

"Oops—what happened? What became of the main course?"

"Mais, monsieur, you just ate it."

"But that's impossible."

"Non, monsieur, see here, the menu, approved by mademoiselle."

It had also been approved by the vice president. Seeing it printed in French on the menu, he had mistakenly believed it was something he had eaten before and had enjoyed.

What could be said at that point, and to whom? The chef had done his job— and well. There was certainly no fault in his preparation. The secretary had done her reliable best—passing on the vice president's instructions exactly as received. She had ordered "something unusual." But, as one of the guests, I can tell you that after a twelve-hour day of meetings, I would have liked something better than SOS, regardless of how nice it sounds in French.

The moral of the story: It's okay to let the chef have his way up to a point, but that point must remain well within the scope of your knowledge—and your ability to communicate clearly.

The speaker's sizzle. As Bud Rebedeau says, "The speaker is the best visual on the stage." And as Elmer Wheeler might have said, "Confidence, believability, and warmth are the sizzle that sells the stories." You can build these ingredients into your presentations by knowing the subject, properly preparing, adequately rehearsing, and letting your audience feel the fire in your soul as you present your convictions.

If you are the speaker, you can self-program to cash in on these attributes. If you're the director, you'll need to bring them out in the speakers. Or, if you are in charge of selecting speakers, you can hire those who best exude these qualities. But, you'll only learn that from seeing them in action—before you sign the contract.

The wrong message for the audience. One of the most embarrassing spectacles I ever sat through happened in 1977. Fortunately, I had nothing to do with the program (actually, I was a participant), but I relearned a valuable lession—in spades.

It was a sizable professional conference. At the last minute, the advertised speaker couldn't make the trip to Houston. On very short notice, the conference leader, through reading a pamphlet, chose a substitute speaker to give the main address on the evening of the banquet.

In casual conversation, he told me what he had done. I asked him if he had ever heard the man before. "No, but he comes highly recommended." As kindly as possible, I told him I thought he was treading on dangerous ground. Privately I thought he was running too high a risk, and I'm sorry to say I was right.

The man was a retired politician and, in fairness, he did have an impressive list of credentials. But when he mounted the speaker's stand, his opening came off lukewarm and went downhill from there. It took a steep nosedive when he started a series of blue jokes.

Whatever the man had going for him was ruined, as far as that group was concerned. Two large contingents of attendees were from the Baptist and Catholic presses. Many of them walked out — as did about one-third of the audience. Those remaining bore his remarks in silence. There was one notable exception, a young woman who stood up and loudly told the speaker that she had had enough of this, was leaving, and anyone else with good sense should follow her example.

Even that didn't slow the speaker down but for a moment. He continued his string of blue jokes for the remaining members of the audience. I walked out for a while, then walked back in — feeling sorry for the speaker, the conference leader, but most of all, for the audience.

As I said earlier, I had nothing to do with this except as an attendee. I did relearn (at the expense of other people) two things I already knew: (1) don't ever hire a speaker sight unseen, who might have been good or might still be good for some audiences, but not yours; and (2) blue humor just does not work in most places.

Backstage communication. Good communication behind the scenes is the glue that holds the meeting together. I know of no better way to stress this than to tell one last tale.

The color wheel. In 1971, I was directing a three-screen, multimedia show in the Astrodome complex in Houston. The presentation was to have an attendance of more than 1000 persons.

We had so many pieces of hardware backstage that we decided to run the show from two programmers. The main part of the show was programmed into a sound-driven one, and all of the accessory equipment was set up on a manually-operated control board.

The stage was set, the technical checks made, and we were ready for our full dress rehearsal. This was no ordinary rehearsal. All of the company big-wigs and some specially invited guests were there to watch us do our stuff.

The way the show was to unfold was with some low-key, walk-in music, then a soft display of lights playing on the center screen. This followed by wilder colors coming up on the two outboard screens, pulsed to the beat of much livelier music . . . then house lights to black and the main show started with a bang—quadraphonic sound—brilliant, colored slides on all screens—a real screamer.

The morning of the rehearsal, the technician for the manual control board was taken sick. An experienced replacement was found and he was checked out quickly on his duties.

I was directing from the rear of the audience, so I could see the show as they saw it. Everyone was seated already, but I began the countdown from the top with a timed chant:

"Everyone on the headsets."

"Check."

"Check."

"Check."

"Check."

"No more cross-talking."

"House lights down half."

The lights receded.

"Start the play-in music."

It began.

"Start the color wheel."

Nothing.

Very calmly, "Start the color wheel."

Nothing.

A little more urgently, "Start the color wheel."

Nothing.

Getting a little testy, "Start the *?#%&!! color wheel!"

Nothing.

I was getting edgy and began figuring my next move. Then, from backstage, came a loud whisper that was heard by the entire audience: "Psst—what the hell is a color wheel?"

The audience couldn't hear me, but after the long pause during which something should have happened, they were clued that there was some difficulty. They broke up laughing.

Somebody straightened out the technician and we began again from the top. This time it was smooth as silk. But, for ten years after, I had people who worked on that show walking up behind me saying, "Psst—what the hell is a color wheel?"

When I went backstage later, I quickly saw the problem. The technician who had been taken ill had neatly labeled all the switches. Written clear as day on the color wheel switch was "pie." I had never heard the expression before, and neither had the substitute technician.

The other big "yuk" in the rehearsal was the coffee break slides. They were in the projector upside down. They were programmed in as part of the show and the audience thought we had intentionally turned them for a laugh. In reality, one of the technicians had taken them out of the tray to show them to somebody on an extra projector; then he had replaced them in the show tray upside down.

Three lessons came out of that rehearsal. One, make sure everyone speaks the same language. Two, do a one-on-one dry run with replacement technicians. And, three, once the show slides are in the tray correctly, lock them in and forbid anyone to touch them.

The Grand Finale

Now is the time to wrap this up. We truly hope we have communicated. Some of our omissions were made intentionally. For example, the mechanics of moving masses of people to, through, and from meetings. We feel that these techniques and others that deal with large conventions and multiday conferences are a book in themselves. We hope to give you such a book in the future.

Our intentions with *this* book are to give you the basics and how-tos of planning and producing successful meetings from a meeting leader's standpoint.

If, after reading our book, you feel there are other topics you would like included in a future edition, please write to us. Or, if you wish to discuss a particular point about meeting planning, either of us is avialable for consultation.

Now, go forth and make sure your meetings are well met!

Glossary of Audiovisual and Camera Terms

AUDIOVISUAL: This term is sometimes hyphenated; the industry itself is not in agreement on whether or not to hyphenate it; often abbreviated A/V or A-V, again with little uniformity. The term is based on the words that refer to hearing and sight; it is used to designate teaching materials and aids such as slides, motion pictures, filmstrips, TV tapes, and various projection and replay equipment.

AUTOMATIC CAMERA: One that measures the light and adjusts itself accordingly.

BUILD: In its simplest form, this is the process of adding lines of type or other step-by-step changes to a series of sequential slides. The slide equivalent of a "reveal" overhead transparency.

BUZZ GROUP A meeting or conference setup in which conference members are divided into small teams or work groups to tackle a project or projects. So called because of the buzzing sound of low conversation that characterizes these groups.

CABLE RELEASE: A shutter release button mounted on a cable. With the cable attached, a camera's shutter can be released remotely. In slide production work on a copystand, the cable release used is about 8 to 12 inches in length.

CAROUSEL: A circular tray for holding 35mm slides in order; also the projector that uses such trays. They are considered exceptionally reliable for making slide presentations since the slides drop by gravity feed.

CHALKBOARD: What we used to call a blackboard is now called a chalkboard because such boards frequently aren't black any more. Indeed, white is a more popular color these days.

CLOSE-UP LENS: Magnifying lenses that screw on the front of a regular lens. Because they screw onto the regular lens, they are sometimes called close-up filters.

COLOR WHEEL: As a color chart, a spectrum of colors arranged chromatically in a circle. The circle arrangement allows easy identification of individual colors and their relationship to the others. As an audiovisual accessory, a spectrum of wedge-shaped colored gels arranged to form a wheel. The center of the wheel is the pivot point. The wheel can be either manually or mechanically rotated in the beam of a projector to create changing colors on a projection screen. The effect is predicated on the speed of rotation.

DEPTH OF FIELD: The amount of photograph that is in focus.

DISSOLVE UNIT: A device for alternately fading in and out the projection beams of two slide projectors being controlled in tandem. The simplest dissolve units are programmed to gradually fade the projection lamp in one projector while gradually increasing the intensity of light from the other projector. This is done during a time-lapse sequence. The effect is that one projected image appears to dissolve while a replacement image (from the opposite projector) constitutes itself on the screen; hence the name dissolve unit. More complex units allow the A/V operator to program the dissolves at a faster or slower rate of speed. Quick cuts (instant slide changes) can also be programmed, or the unit can be reversed.

f-**SCALE:** A scale of various aperture settings for a camera.

f-**STOP:** An aperture setting.

FILMSTRIP: A continuous roll or strip of 35mm film onto which a series of slides has been transferred. Sometimes they are accompanied by a sound track (usually on tape), which sends an inaudible signal to the projector to advance each frame. With a continuous film loop, such a projector can function unattended.

FILTER: Any attachment that screws onto the front of a camera lens. Usually used to filter out certain colors.

FIXED LENS: A nonadjustable lens with a preset focus. Also called a simple lens.

FLIPCHART: A series of large sheets of paper, in pad form, on which items of information can be prepared in advance or on the spot and shown to an audience one step at a time.

FOCAL LENGTH: One measurement of the internal optics of a lens. Rather than try to explain the very complicated formula for determining focal length, let me tell you the practical importance of this. The longer the focal length of a lens, the larger the image you are photographing will appear on the film. This is why long focal length lenses are usually referred to as telephoto lenses.

FRESNEL LENS: A very flat projection lens made up of a series of much smaller lenses that appear to the naked eye as grooves inscribed in the surface. A key component in overhead projectors, forming the light table.

GEL: A transparent film in color; used to tint lights or placed over artwork to change white or light colors to a different shade or tint.

KEYSTONING: Distortion in a projected image, resulting when the projector is not lined up at exactly right angles to the screen.

LECTERN: A stand for holding the notes, written speech, etc., of a speaker or lecturer. The word "podium" is frequently misused to mean lectern.

MACROLENS: A lens that can provide 1 to 1 magnification or can be adjusted for use as a normal-length lens.

MOCK-UP: Somewhat like a model except that it does not have to be an exact copy of the original; it may contain only the particular parts to be studied or discussed; these may be enlarged in detail or, in many cases, highly simplified. A mock-up may or may not have moving parts.

MODEL: A three-dimensional copy or facsimile designed to show every part and detail of the original, with the prime difference being that of size. A model is usually scaled down (or sometimes up) by a specific ratio.

OVERHEAD PROJECTION: A system for projecting art prepared on transparent film onto a screen, using a very short "throw" (distance from the lens to the screen). Most such projectors employ a Fresnel lens for the light table on which the transparency is placed. The projectionist can simply show the transparency as is, or has the option of writing or drawing on the transparent film surface, or using other techniques such as the reveal.

For some reason, the equipment and the medium lend themselves to a variety of nicknames or slang terms. Often the projector is simply called an overhead. The transparencies are called, in various geographical locations, overheads, overhead cells, cells, overhead transparencies, viewgraphs, and slinkies. (We're both guilty of continuing to confuse this issue by using all of these terms—except slinky—in various references in the text. Our apologies.)

PC CORD: The power cord that connects a flash unit to a camera.

PANTOGRAPH: A mechanical device consisting of a framework of joined rods in a roughly parallelogram form; used to reproduce drawings, letters, etc., on the same or a different scale.

PODIUM: This word, much misused and abused, is related to the Greek word for foot. It means a low platform, especially for the conductor of an orchestra or a speaker to stand on. It is frequently confused with the word lectern.

PROGRAMMER: A control unit for regulating the functions of multiple pieces of audio-visual equipment. Usually sound-activated, the programmer is constructed so each time it is advanced it completes one function: turns on equipment, changes a slide, advances the dissolve unit, turns off equipment, and so on. Almost any standard piece of A/V equipment can be plugged into the programmer. Programmer prices range from a few hundred dollars up to several thousand. Generally, the more expensive the programmer, the more pieces of equipment it can control.

REAR-SCREEN PROJECTION: A system for projecting films or slides (in reverse) from behind a translucent screen, with the result that viewers in front of the screen see the picture in its proper arrangement. This setup is useful for showing projected material in a relatively well-lighted room.

SEQUENCE: A series of slides used in specific order to tell a story.

SHUTTER RELEASE: The button or lever that trips the shutter on a camera.

SHUTTER SPEED: The amount of time that a camera lets in the light, measured in fractions of a second (a speed of 500 = $\frac{1}{500}$ second).

SLIDE PROJECTOR: A device for projecting a beam of high-intensity light through a photographic transparency, focusing it through a lens, and reproducing the projected image on a reflective surface (screen). As referred to in this book, one which projects standard 35mm slides. Although there are a number of manufacturers of this equipment, we have referred to only two types by name, Carousel and Ektagraphic, both Kodak brand names.

SLIDE PROJECTOR REMOTE CONTROL: A hand-held control device used to advance, reverse, or focus a slide projector. In slang, it is sometimes called a pickle switch.

SLIDES: A film transparency mounted for projection in a slide projector. In this book, all slides mentioned (unless otherwise noted) are standard 35mm. At one time, *lantern slide* was the term used to describe all slides. Today, this term is generally reserved for larger than standard transparencies. A common transparency size of lantern slide is 3.25 x 3 inches. The Polaroid lantern transparency is even larger (3.25 x 3.4 inches). A *super slide* is a slide that has a mount of the same outside dimensions as found on a 35mm slide, but with a projection surface ⅝ inch larger.

SOUND/SLIDE PROGRAM: A slide show with mechanically reproduced narration and/or sound effects. Operation of the program requires an audio tape playback unit and a slide projector. Generally the tape is beeped or pulsed to trigger slide changes in the projector (a mechanical program), or an operator can manually trigger slide changes.

TELEPHOTO LENS: In general terminology, any lens that is longer than normal for that particular camera, or a lens with a long focal length.

VIDEODISC: An A/V recording system in which sound and picture signals are recorded on the surface of a disc whose appearance is somewhat like that of a phonograph record. Picture and sound quality are excellent; however, discs cannot be recorded by the user. Like commercial phonograph records, they must be purchased with the program already inscribed on the disc. Several different methods of recording are now fighting it out in the marketplace.

VIDEOTAPE: A recording medium capable of inscribing both audio (sound) and video (picture) onto a strip of magnetic tape. Tapes come in various sizes and configurations, ranging from 2-inch and 1-inch broadcast quality, to ¾-inch "U-matic" format used by most training professionals, to the home-type Beta and VHS systems that use ½-inch tape cassettes and produce pictures of somewhat lower quality.

VOICEOVER: The voice on a mechanically reproduced sound track or a live voice of an unseen narrator.

WIDE ANGLE: A lens of a shorter focal length than the normal lens for that particular camera.

ZOOM LENS: A lens of variable focal length.

Bibliography

Audiovisual and Photography

American Society for Training and Development: *Media Resource Directory,* ASTD Publishing Services, Baltimore, Md. (annual).

Anderson, Ronald H.: *Selecting and Developing Media for Instruction,* American Society for Training and Development, Madison, Wis., 1976.

Beatty, LaMond F.: *Filmstrips,* Educational Technology Publications, Englewood Cliffs, N.J., 1981.

Bill Daniels Company, The: *Illustrated Media Reference,* Shawnee Mission, Kans. (annual).

Bowker, R. R. Company: *Audiovisual Market Place,* New York (annual).

Brown, James W., R. B. Lewis, and Fred F. Harcleroad: *AV Instruction: Media and Methods,* McGraw-Hill, New York, 1973.

Brown, James W. and Richard B. Lewis: *AV Instructional Materials Manual: A Self-Instructional Guide to AV Laboratory Experiences,* 3d ed., McGraw-Hill, New York, 1969.

Brown, James W. and Kenneth D. Norberg: *Administering Educational Media: Instructional Technology and Library Services,* 2d ed., McGraw-Hill, New York, 1972.

Bunyan, John A., James C. Crimmins, and N. Kyri Watson: *Practical Video,* Knowledge Industry Publications, White Plains, N.Y., 1978.

Bunyan, John and James Crimmins: *Television Management, The Manager's Guide to Video,* Knowledge Industry Publications, White Plains, N.Y., 1977.

Burden, Ernest E.: *Visual Presentation,* Big G Press, New York, 1977.

Culclasure, David F.: *Effective Use of Audiovisual Media,* Prentice-Hall, Englewood Cliffs, N.J., 1969.

Dale, Edgar: *Audiovisual Methods in Teaching,* Dryden Press, New York, 1969.

DeKieffer, Robert E.: *Audiovisual Instruction,* Center for Applied Research in Education, New York, 1965.

DeKieffer, Robert E. and Lee W. Cochran: *Manual of Audio-Visual Techniques,* Prentice-Hall, Englewood Cliffs, N.J., 1962.

Diamond, Robert M. (ed.): *A Guide to Instructional Television,* McGraw-Hill, New York, 1964.

Dwyer, Francis M.: *Strategies for Improving Visual Learning,* Learning Services, State College, Penn., 1978.

Eboch, Sidney C.: *Operating Audio-Visual Equipment,* Chandler, San Francisco, 1968.

Educational Media Council: *Educational Media Index,* McGraw-Hill, New York, 1964.

Erickson, Carlton W. H.: *Administering Instructional Media Programs,* Macmillan, New York, 1968.

Erickson, Carlton W. and David H. Curl: *Fundamentals of Teaching with Audiovisual Technology,* 2d ed., Macmillan, New York, 1972.

Forsdale, Louis (ed.): *8mm Sound Film and Education,* Bureau of Publications, Teachers College, Columbia University, New York, 1962.

Foster, Roy: *Communications, Control, Decision Making and Training With Television,* R. Foster, Glasgow, Scotland, 1968.

Godfrey, Eleanor P.: *The State of Audiovisual Technology 1961–1966,* Monograph No. 3, Department of Audiovisual Instruction, National Education Association, Washington, D.C., 1967.

Goudket, Michael: *Audiovisual Primer* (rev. ed.), Teachers College Press, New York, 1974.

Green, Alan C., et al.: *Educational Facilities with New Media,* Department of Audiovisual Instruction, National Education Association, Washington, D.C., 1966.

Gropper, George Leonard: *Criteria for the Selection and Use of Visuals in Instruction,* Educational Technology Publications, Englewood Cliffs, N.J., 1971.

Haas, Kenneth Brooks: *Preparation and Use of Audio-Visual Aids,* Prentice-Hall, New York, 1955.

Hamer, K. W.: *American Association of Management Bulletin 28,* "Making the Most of Charts," AT&T Business Research Division, New York, 1960.

Hartsell, Horace C. and W. L. Veenendaal: *Overhead Projection,* Henry Stewart, Buffalo, N.Y., 1965.

Hemp, Jerrold E., et al., *Planning and Producing Audiovisual Materials,* 3d ed., Thomas Y. Crowell, New York, 1975.

Hitchens, Howard (ed.): *Producing Slide and Tape Presentations,* Association for Educational Communications and Technology, Washington, D.C., 1980.

Horkheimer, Mary Foley and John C. Diffor: *Educator's Guide to Free Films,* Educators Progress Service, Randolph, Wis. (annual).

Horkheimer, Mary Foley and John C. Diffor: *Educator's Guide to Free Filmstrips,* Educators Progress Service, Randolph, Wis. (annual).

Horn, George F.: *Visual Communication: Bulletin Boards, Exhibits, Visual Aids,* Davis Publications, Worcester, Mass., 1973.

Individual Welfare Society: *Using Sound Filmstrips,* London, 1962.

Kemp, Jerrold E.: *Planning and Producing Audiovisual Materials,* Chandler Publishing, Scranton, Penn., 1968.

Korete, D. A.: *Television in Education and Training,* Centrex, Eindhoven, Netherlands, 1967.

Kueter, Roger A.: *Slides,* Educational Technology Publications, Englewood Cliffs, N.J., 1981.

Lamb, Brydon: *Filmstrips and Slide Projectors in Teaching and Training,* National Committee for Audio-Visual Aids in Education, Educational Foundation for the Visual Arts, London, 1971.

Lansford, John: *Visual Aids and Photography in Education,* Hastings House Publishers, New York, 1973.

McGraw-Hill: *Practical Charting Techniques,* McGraw-Hill, New York, 1969.

McLuhan, Marshall: *Understanding Media,* McGraw-Hill, New York, 1964.

Minor, Edward and Harvey R. Frye: *Techniques for Producing Visual Instructional Media,* McGraw-Hill, New York, 1970.

Morrisey, George I.: *Effective Business and Technical Presentations,* Addison-Wesley Publishing Company, Reading, Mass., 1968.

Murgio, Matthew P.: *Communications Graphics,* Van Nostrand Reinhold, New York, 1969.

Murphy, Judith and Ronald Gross, *Learning by Television,* Fund for the Advancement of Education, New York, 1966.

National Audio-Visual Association, Inc.: *Audio-Visual Equipment Directory,* Fairfax, Va. (annual).

National Audio-Visual Association, Inc.: *Audio-Visual Membership Directory,* Fairfax, Va. (annual).

Nelms, Henning: *Thinking With a Pencil,* Barnes and Noble, New York, 1964.

Nelson, Leslie W.: *Instructional Aids and How to Make and Use Them,* Wm. C. Brown, Dubuque, Iowa, 1970.

Parker, Norton S.: *Audiovisual Script Writing,* Rutgers University Press, New Brunswick, N.J., 1968.

Pula, Fred John: *Application and Operation of Audiovisual Equipment in Education,* Wiley, New York, 1968.

Quick, John and Herbert Wolff: *Small-Studio Video Tape Production,* Addison-Wesley, Reading, Mass., 1972.

Quinley, William J.: *The Selection, Acquisition, and Utilization of Audiovisual Materials,* Information Futures, Pullman, Washington, D.C., 1978.

Rigg, Robinson Peter: *Audiovisual Aids and Techniques in Managerial and Supervisory Training,* Hamilton, London, 1969.

Riggleman, John R.: *Graphic Methods for Presenting Business Statistics,* 2d ed., McGraw-Hill, 1936.

Roberts, Martin: *Video Cassettes: The Systems, The Market, The Future,* Martin Roberts & Associates, Beverly Hills, Calif., 1970.

Rogers, Anna C.: *Graphics Charts Handbook,* Public Affairs Press, Washington, D.C., 1961.

Romiszowski, A. J.: *Selection and Use of Instructional Media,* Halsted Press, Division of John Wiley & Sons, New York, 1974.

Rossi, Peter H. and Bruce J. Biddle: *The New Media and Education,* Aldine, Chicago, 1966.

Rothschild, Norman: *Making Slide Duplicates, Titles and Filmstrips,* 3d ed., Amphoto, New York, 1973.

Schmid, Calvin: *Handbook of Graphic Presentation,* Ronald, New York, 1954.

Smart, Edwin L. and Sam Arnold: *Practical Rules for Graphic Presentation of Business Statistics,* O.S.U. Bureau of Business Research, Research Monograph 46, Columbus, Ohio, 1951.

Spear, Mary Eleanor: *Charting Statistics,* McGraw-Hill, New York, 1972.

Sylvania Electric Products, Inc.: *Sylvania Lighting Handbook for Television, Theatre, Professional Photography,* Danvers, Mass., 1969.

Tanzmann, Jack and Kenneth J. Dunn: *Using Instructional Media Effectively,* Prentice-Hall, Englewood Cliffs, N.J., 1971.

Taylor, Calvin and Frank E. Williams (eds.): *Instructional Media and Creativity,* Wiley, New York, 1966.

Thornton, James W. Jr. and James W. Brown: *New Media and College Teaching,* Department of Audiovisual Instruction, National Education Association, Washington, D.C., 1968.

3M Company, Magnetic Products Division: *Better Communications Through Tape,* St. Paul, Minn., 1968.

Travers, Robert M. W.: *Studies Related to the Design of Audiovisual Teaching Materials,* U.S. Office of Education, Washington, D.C., 1966.

Weld, Walter C.: *How to Chart,* Codex, Norwood, Mass., 1959.

Wileman, Ralph E.: *Exercises in Visual Thinking,* Hastings House, New York, 1979.

Williams, Catherine M.: *Learning from Pictures,* Department of Audiovisual Instruction, National Education Association, Washington, D.C., 1963.

Wittich, Walter A. and Raymond H. Suttles: *Educator's Guide to Free Tapes, Scripts, and Transcriptions,* Educators Progress Service, Randolph, Wis. (annual).

Wittich, Walter A. and Charles F. Schuller: *Instructional Technology: Its Nature and Use,* 5th ed., Harper & Row, New York, 1975.

Eastman Kodak Publications

For a complete list, send for *Index to Kodak Information* (L-5), Eastman Kodak Company, Department 412-L, Rochester, New York 14650.

A Simple Wooden Copying Stand for Making Title Slides and Filmstrips, 1976.

A Way To Do It Better, 1978.

Audiovisual Literature Packet

Audiovisual Notes from Kodak—Professional Presentation, Minimum Cost (in 2 parts), 1977.

Audiovisual Notes from Kodak—Visualizing Your Way to a Script; 101 Ways to Make Copy and Title Slides, Part III; Buying Title Slides, 1979.

Audiovisual Notes from Kodak—Where Do Visual Ideas Come From, and How Do You Keep Them Alive?, 1977.

Audiovisual Planning Equipment, 1979.

Audiovisual Projection

Basic Art Techniques for Slide Production

Basic Copying

Basic 2 x 2-inch Slide Packet, 1980.

Black-and-White Transparencies with Kodak Panatomic-X Film, 1977.

Copying

Effective Lecture Slides, 1977.

Effective Visual Presentations

How to Make Good Pictures

Images, Images, Images—The Book of Programmed Multi-Image Production, Michael F. Kenny and Raymond F. Schmitt, 1979.

Kodak Projection Calculator and Seating Guide

Legibility—Artwork to Screen, 1977.

Making Black-and-White or Color Transparencies for Overhead Projection, 1975.

Materials for Visual Presentations—Planning and Preparation, 1978.

Movies with a Purpose, 1968.

Multi-Image Production Packet, 1980.

Planning and Producing Slide Programs, 1978.

Planning and Producing Visual Aids, 1969.

Projection Distance Tables for Kodak Ektagraphic and Carousel Slide Projectors

Reflection Characteristics of Front-Projection Screen Materials

Reverse-Text Slides, 1979.

Simple Copying Techniques with a Kodak Ektagraphic Visualmaker

Slides With a Purpose, 1977.

Speechmaking . . . More Than Words Alone, 1979.

Synchronizing a Slide/Tape Program

Using Polarized Light for Copying, 1979.

Wide Screen and Multiple Screen Presentations

Group Discussion, Communication, and Problem Solving

Adams, James L.: *Conceptual Blockbusting*, W. H. Freeman, San Francisco, 1974.

Anastasi, Thomas E.: *Desk Guide to Communication*, Devlin House, Medfield, Mass., 1974.

Applbaum, Ronald L., Edward M. Bodaken, Kenneth L. Sereno, and Karl W. E. Anatol: *The Process of Group Communication*, Science Research Associates, Chicago, 1974.

Auer, John Jeffrey: *Handbook for Discussion Leaders,* Greenwood Press, Westport, Conn., 1974.

Burgoon, Michael and Michael Ruffner: *Human Communication,* Holt, Rinehart, and Winston, New York, 1978.

Cathcart, Robert S.: *Small Group Communication,* W. C. Brown, Dubuque, Iowa, 1979.

Chamber of Commerce of the United States of America: *Developing Business Leadership Through Economic Discussion Groups,* Washington, D.C., 1973.

Chenoweth, Eugene Clay: *Discussion and Debate,* W. C. Brown, Dubuque, Iowa, 1951.

Curtis, Dan B.: *Communication for Problem-Solving,* Wiley, New York, 1979.

Downs, Cal W.: *The Organizational Communicator,* Harper & Row, New York, 1977.

Eddy, William B. et al.: *Behavioral Science and the Manager's Role,* NTL Institute, Fairfax, Va., 1969.

Gordon, Thomas: *Group-Centered Leadership,* Houghton-Mifflin, Boston, 1955.

Gordon, W. J. J.: *Synectics,* Harper & Row, New York, 1961.

Harnack, Robert Victor: *Group Discussion,* Prentice-Hall, Englewood Cliffs, N.J., 1977.

Hasling, John: *Group Discussion and Decision Making,* Crowell, New York, 1975.

Interaction Associates: *Strategy Notebook,* Interaction Associates, San Francisco, 1972.

Janis, Irving: *Victims of Groupthink,* Houghton-Mifflin, Boston, 1972.

Jones, Stanley E.: *The Dynamics of Discussion,* Harper & Row, New York, 1978.

Jorgensen, James D.: *Solving Problems in Meetings,* Nelson-Hall, Chicago, 1981.

Kaberg, Don and Tom Bagnell: *The Universal Traveler,* William Kaufmann, Los Altos, Calif., 1972.

Kemp, C. Gratton: *Perspectives on the Group Process,* Houghton-Mifflin, Boston, 1964.

Luft, Joseph: *Group Processes,* National Press Books, Palo Alto, Calif., 1963.

McKim, Robert H.: *Experience in Visual Thinking,* Brooks/Cole Publishing Company, Monterey, Calif., 1972.

McPherson, J. H.: *The People, the Problems, and the Problem Solving Methods,* The Pendall Company, Midland, Mich., 1967.

Miles, Matthew: *Learning to Work in Groups,* Teachers College Press, New York, 1969.

Newstrom, John W. and Edward Scannell: *Games Trainers Play: Experiential Learning Exercises,* McGraw-Hill, New York, 1980.

Parnes, S. J.: *Creative Behavior Guidebook,* Scribner, New York, 1967.

Patton, Bobb R. and Kim Griffin: *Problem Solving Group Interaction,* Harper & Row, New York, 1973.

Phillips, Gerald M.: *Group Discussion, a Practical Guide to Participation and Leadership,* Houghton-Mifflin, Boston, 1979.

Prince, George M.: *The Practice of Creativity,* Collier, New York, 1972.

Rawlinson, J. G.: *Creative Thinking and Brainstorming,* Wiley, New York, 1981.

Rickards, Tudor: *Problem-Solving Through Creative Analysis,* Wiley, New York, 1973.

Rooks, George: *The Non-Stop Discussion Workbook,* Newberry House, Rowley, Mass., 1981.

Rothwell, J. Dan and James I. Costigan: *Interpersonal Communication,* Charles E. Merrill, Columbus, Ohio, 1975.

Sattler, William M. and N. Edd Miller: *Discussion and Conference,* 2d ed., Prentice-Hall, Englewood Cliffs, N.J., 1968.

Scheidel, Thomas Maynard: *Discussing and Deciding,* Macmillan, New York, 1979.

Schein, E. and W. Bennis: *Personal & Organizational Change Through Group Methods: The Laboratory Approach,* Wiley, New York, 1965.

Smith, William S.: *Group Problem-Solving Through Discussion,* Bobbs-Merrill, Indianapolis, 1965.

Steiner, Ivan D.: *Group Process and Productivity,* Academic, New York, 1972.

Tropman, John E.: *The Essentials of Committee Management,* Nelson-Hall, Chicago, 1979.

Webb, Ewing and John B. Morgan: *Strategy in Handling People,* Halcyon, Garden City, N.Y., 1948.

Meetings: Planning and Conducting

AMACOM: *Conference Leadership,* New York, 1972.

American Society of Association Executives: *Making Your Convention More Effective,* Washington, D.C., 1972.

Auger, B. Y.: *How to Find Better Business Meeting Places,* Business Services Press, St. Paul, Minn., 1966.

Auger, B. Y.: *How to Run Better Business Meetings: An Executive's Guide to Meetings that Get Things Done,* 8th ed., 3M Company, St. Paul, Minn., 1979.

Beiber, Marion: *How to Run a Conference,* Allen & Unwin, London, 1968.

Bell, Chip and Frederic Margolis: *A Presenter's Guide to Conferences,* American Society for Training and Development.

Bradford, Leland P.: *Making Meetings Work: A Guide for Leaders and Group Members,* University Associates, San Diego, 1976.

Bureau of Naval Personnel, U.S. Navy: *Conference Sense,* NavPers 91139, Washington, D.C., 1950.

Burke, Wyatt Warner: *Conference Planning,* NTL Institute for Applied Behavioral Science, Washington, D.C., 1970.

Burke, Wyatt Warner and Richard Beckhard (eds.): *Conference Planning,* 2d ed., University Associates, San Diego, 1976.

Cavalier, Richard: *Achieving Objectives in Meetings,* Program Counsel, New York, 1973.

Dartnell Corporation: *Conducting Better Sales Meetings,* Chicago, 1964.

DeVoe, Merrill: *Modern Techniques for Conducting Effective Meetings,* EMD Publications, Lexington, Ken., 1968.

Doyle, Michael and David Straus: *How to Make Meetings Work,* Playboy Press, New York, 1977.

Drain, Robert H.: *Successful Conference and Convention Planning,* McGraw-Hill, New York, 1978.

Dun and Bradstreet Business Library: *How to Conduct a Meeting,* Thomas Y. Crowell, Scranton, Penn., 1970.

Dunsing, Richard J.: *You and I Have Simply Got to Stop Meeting This Way,* AMACOM, New York, 1978.

Favreau, Donald F.: *Planning and Conducting Successful Meetings and Conferences,* Lane Press of Albany, Albany, N.Y., 1970.

Finkel, Coleman: *How to Plan Meetings Like a Professional,* SM/Sales Meetings Magazine, Philadelphia, 1972.

Finkel, Coleman: *Professional Guide to Successful Meetings,* Herman Publishing, Boston, 1976.

Gertsner, Merrill: *Sales Meetings That Sell,* AMACOM, New York, 1973.

Hart, Lois Borland: *A Conference and Workshop Planner's Manual,* AMACOM, New York, 1979.

Hegarty, Edward J.: *How to Run Better Meetings,* McGraw-Hill, New York, 1957.

Hoge, Carol S.: *Better Meetings: A Handbook for Trainers of Policy Councils and Other Decision-Making Groups,* Humanics Associates, Atlanta, 1975.

Hon, David: *Meetings That Matter,* Wiley, New York, 1980.

Insurance Conference Planners Association: *Convention Check List and Meeting Plan,* Meeting Planners International, Chicago (undated).

Jeffries, James R.: *Meetings: Where, Why, How to ... ,* The Coca-Cola Company, Foods Division, Houston, 1978.

Jones, James E.: *All About ... Hotel Negotiations,* Meeting Planners International, Chicago (undated).

Jones, James E.: *Meeting Management: A Professional Approach,* Bayard Publications, Stamford, Conn., 1979.

Jones, Martin: *How to Organize Meetings,* Beaufort Books, New York, 1981.

John J. Kielty Company: *How to Plan and Conduct Successful Sales Meetings,* Dartnell Corporation, Chicago, 1967.

Kirkpatrick, Donald L.: *How to Plan and Conduct Productive Business Meetings,* Dartnell Corporation, Chicago, 1976.

Lobinger, John: *Business Meetings that Make Business,* Macmillan, Riverside, N.J., 1969.

Long, Fern: *All About Meetings,* Oceana Publications, Dobbs Ferry, N.Y., 1967.

Loughary, John W. and Barrie Hopson: *Producing Workshops, Seminars, and Short Courses,* Association Press/Follett, Chicago, 1979.

Madsen, Paul O.: *The Person Who Chairs the Meeting,* Judson Press, Valley Forge, Penn., 1973.

Morris, Jack R.: *How to Run a Convention Without Losing Your Mind,* Incentive Publications, Dallas, 1977.

Nadler, Leonard and Zeace Nadler: *The Conference Book: How to Successfully Design, Plan, Staff, and Run Conferences of 25 or More People,* Gulf Publishing Company, Houston, 1977.

Nathan, E. D.: *Twenty Questions on Conference Leadership,* Addison-Wesley, Reading, Mass., 1969.

National Association of Attorney Generals: *Open Meetings,* Office of Attorney General, Raleigh, N.C., 1979.

Preston Publishing Company, Inc.: *How to Contribute to Business Meetings,* New York, (undated).

Public Management Institute: *Successful Seminars, Conferences, and Workshops,* San Francisco, 1980.

Queen's Printer, Canadian Citizenship Branch: *The Art of Program Planning,* Ottawa, 1967.

Redden, Martha R., et al.: *Barrier-Free Meetings: A Guide for Professional Associations,* American Association for the Advancement of Science, Washington, D.C., 1976.

Renton, Michael: *Getting Better Results From the Meetings You Run,* Research Press, Champaign, Ill., 1980.

SM/Sales Meeting Magazine: *The Theory and Practice of Convention Management,* Philadelphia, 1969.

Schindler-Rainman, Eva and Ronald Lippit: *Taking Your Meetings Out of the Doldrums,* University Associates, San Diego, 1975.

Skelly, Olive Kathleen: *Conference Planning and Administration,* Industrial Society, London, 1966.

Snell, Frank: *How to Hold a Better Meeting,* Cornerstone Library, New York, 1976.

Stanford, Geoffrey: *Conduct of Meetings,* Oxford University Press, Fair Lawn, N.J., 1958.

Steinkrauss, W.: *Conference Planning*, Ministry of Community and Social Services, Toronto, 1973.

Taylor, Helen Margaret: *The Right Way to Conduct Meetings, Conferences, and Discussions*, Elliot Right Way Books, Kingswood, England, 1968.

This, Leslie E.: *The Small Meeting Planner*, Gulf Publishing Company, Houston, 1972.

3M Company: *Conference Room Planning Guide*, St. Paul, Minn. (undated).

3M Company: *The How-To's of Successful International Meetings*, Visual Products Division, St. Paul, Minn., 1979.

Tropman, John E.: *Effective Meetings*, published in cooperation with the Continuing Education Program in the Human Services of the University of Michigan School of Social Work, Beverly Hills, Calif., 1980.

Zelko, Harold P.: *The Business Conference: Leadership and Participation*, McGraw-Hill, New York, 1969.

Zelko, Harold P.: *Successful Conference and Discussion Techniques*, McGraw-Hill, New York, 1957.

Ziff-Davis Publishing Company, Inc.: *Official Meeting Facilities Guide*, New York (annual).

Speechmaking and Speechwriting

Andersen, Martin P., E. Ray Nichols, and Herbert W. Booth: *The Speaker and His Audience*, Harper & Row, New York, 1974.

Barker, Thoburn V.: *The Speech: Its Structure and Composition*, American Book, New York, 1968.

Brown, Ronald Michael: *Practical Speechmaking*, W. C. Brown, Dubuque, Iowa, 1970.

Connelly, J. Campbell: *A Manager's Guide to Speaking and Listening*, American Management Association, New York, 1967.

Handley, Cathy: *Ten Days to Miracle Speech Power*, Prentice-Hall, Englewood Cliffs, N.J., 1978.

Hawnes, Jady L.: *Organizing a Speech*, Prentice-Hall, Englewood Cliffs, N.J., 1981.

Howell, William S. and Ernest G. Bormann: *Presentational Speaking for Business and the Professions*, Harper & Row, Scranton, Penn., 1971.

Jay, Anthony: *The New Oratory*, American Management Association, New York, 1971.

Kaye, Philip: *Preparing Speeches of Substance*, Wesleyan Press, Lincoln, Neb., 1969.

Kelley, Joseph J.: *Speechwriting*, Stackpole Books, Harrisburg, Penn., 1981.

Leth, Pamela C.: *Public Communication*, Cummings, Menlo Park, Calif., 1977.

Mohrmann, G. P.: *Composition and Style in the Writing of Speeches*, W. C. Brown, Dubuque, Iowa, 1970.

Mouat, Lawrence Henry: *To Make a Speech*, Pacific Books, Palo Alto, Calif., 1966.

Nash, John: *How to Write and Deliver a Speech*, Trident Press, New York, 1970.

Quick, John: *I Hate to Make Speeches: Help for People Who Must*, Grosset & Dunlap, New York, 1973.

Rodman, George: *Speaking Out: Message Preparation for Professionals*, Holt, Rinehart, and Winston, New York, 1978.

Rogge, Edward and James C. Ching: *Advanced Public Speaking*, Holt, Rinehart, and Winston, New York, 1966.

Ullman, Louis L.: *Writing for Flexible Oral Presentation*, Stanford Research Institute, Huntsville, Ala., 1968.

Wallace, Karl Richards: *Understanding Discourse*, Louisiana State University Press, Baton Rouge, 1971.

Zelko, Harold P. and Frank E. X. Dance: *Business and Professional Speech Communication,* 2d ed., Holt, Rinehart, and Winston, New York, 1978.

Periodicals

AV Guide: The Learning Media Magazine, Trade Periodicals, Chicago.
Audio-Visual Communication Review, National Education Association, Washington, D.C.
Audio-Visual Communications, United Business Publications, New York.
Audio-Visual Department Store Catalog, The, Visual Horizons, Rochester, New York.
Audiovisual Instruction, Association for Educational Communication and Technology, Washington, D.C.
Audiovisual Instruction, National Education Association, Washington, D.C.
Backstage, Backstage Publications, New York.
Business Screen, Chicago.
Conference World, Association of Conference Executives, Huntingdon, England.
Educational Screen and Audio-Visual Guide, Chicago.
Educational Technology, Saddle Brook, N.J.
EPIE Forum, New York.
Meetings and Conventions, Ziff-Davis Publishing Company, New York.
Meetings and Expositions, Morristown, N.J.
Meetings & Incentive Travel, Southam Communications, Ontario, Canada.
News Letter, Ohio State University, Bureau of Educational Research, Columbus, Ohio.
Toastmaster, The, Toastmasters International, Santa Ana, Calif.
Training: The Magazine of Human Resources Development, Lakewood Publications, Minneapolis.
Training and Development, American Society for Training and Development, Washington, D.C.
Training World, Vanderbilt Communications Company, New York.
Visual Education, National Committee for Audio-Visual Aids in Education, London.

Index

Index

■

Cameras (*Cont.*):
  hand-held operation, 161
  lenses (*see* Lenses, camera)
  PC cords, 166
  tripods and substitutes for, 161
Cape Kennedy (NASA), 51–52, 59–60,
    66–67
Catering office, dealing with, 18–19
Cells, overhead (transparencies), 132–
    135
  adding color to, 133
  layout and design, 133–134
  overlays with 153–157
  "reveal" technique, 153, 183
Chalkboards, 49–51
  magnetic, 50
Check-in packets for guests, 34
Checklists:
  fitting graphics to communications, 45
  group meeting requirements summary,
    35–36
  instructional materials, 88
  leader's, 82–85
  meeting room, 17–18
  for restrooms (City of Houston's stan-
    dards for), 20
Chinese method of planning, 38
Choosing cameras, criteria for, 158–161
Choosing the room and the site (for
    meetings), 13–21
Choosing seating arrangements, 24–27
Choosing visual aids, 44
Clarification, visual supports for, 38–39
Clip art, 150
Cocktail parties, 33–34
Coffee breaks, 18
Color, use of, in visual aids, 54
Color wheel, 201–203
Competition among teams, 27
"Conference Leader's Guide," 84
Conference style of seating arrangement,
    26
Conflict, meeting to resolve, 8–10
  work-related, 8
Consultants, use of, 9–10
  criteria for choosing, 10
  in problem solving, 9–10
Contracts, handling, 191–192
Controling the environment (*see* Environ-
    ment, control of)
Controlled exposure (in camera film),
    159
Cooling and heating of meeting rooms,
    16–17

Copying machines, 195
Copystands, 166, 172–177
  choosing, 172
  setting up, 173–174
Cost of meetings, 2–3
  hidden costs, 2

Delivery of speeches, 74–76
Die-cut lettering, 143–144
Directed discussion, 83
Directed reading, 81
Directed writing, 81
Directions, specific, importance of, 21
Discussion:
  directed, 83
  as training technique, 83
  (*See also* Discussion groups)
Discussion groups, 26–27, 82
Display boards for storyboards, 112–113
"Dissolves" (slides), 124
Distractions in presentations, 41
"Do-it-yourself" visuals, 132–138
Doyle, Sir Arthur Conan (quotation), 116
Dressing up visuals, 116–118
Drink (alcoholic beverages), 32–34
  "by the bottle," 32
  "corkage charge," 33–34
  "per drink," 33
Dry-transfer letters, 140–141

Electronic media, 46, 54–63
Emerson, Ralph Waldo (quotation), 30
Environment, control of, 16–17
  ambiance, 16
  checklist for, 17–18
  furniture arrangement, 16, 17, 24–27
  lighting, 17
  sound (wanted and unwanted), 17
  temperature (heating and cooling), 16,
    17
Equipment failure, backups for, 194
Exciter lamps (sound head), 61
Exercises as teaching aids, 82
Extension cords, importance of, 195
Eye contact, importance of, in speaking,
    74
Eye movement, 74

f-stop settings in cameras, 159–161
  "bracketing" technique, 176
Facial expression of speakers, 74–75

■

■

About the Authors

JAMES R. JEFFRIES brings to this book the practical, hands-on experience of having written or directed at least 6 motion pictures, 20 TV tapes, 200 speeches, and 150 sound/slide programs. He has over a decade of experience as a speaker, training director, and meeting planner for the Foods Division of The Coca-Cola Company, where he coordinated and stage-managed meetings for as many as 1200 people. He now runs his own consulting firm in training and communications.

JEFFERSON D. BATES specializes in communications skills as president of his own firm. Author of the widely acclaimed *Writing with Precision*, he has more than 30 years experience as a professional writer. He served as one of the first editorial directors of the U.S. Air Force "Effective Writing Program" in the 1950s and as NASA's chief ghostwriter for more than a decade during the manned space flight program. Hard on the heels of his newly published *Dictating Effectively* is Mr. Bates' work-in-progress, *The Professional Speechwriter*, based on his experience with NASA.